Church Pocket Book and Diary 2024

with Lectionary

Personal memoranda

Name ....

Address (home) ....

....

....

Telephone ....

Mobile ....

Email ....

Address (work) ....

....

....

Telephone ....

Email ....

Blood group ....

In case of emergency please notify: ....

Name ....

Address ....

....

....

Telephone ....

Mobile ....

Email ....

Church Pocket Book and Diary 2024
ISBN 978-0-281-08958-1 (Black)
ISBN 978-0-281-08959-8 (Navy Floral)

Printed in Türkiye by Mega Basim

Contents

Calendar 2024

JANUARY

Su	.	B	E^2	E^3	E^4	..
M	1	8	15	22	29	..
TU	2	9	16	23	30	..
W	3	10	17	24	31	..
TH	4	11	18	25	..	..
F	5	12	19	26	..	..
Sa	E	13	20	27	..	..

FEBRUARY

Su	.	L^{-2}	L^{-1}	L^1	L^2	..
M	.	5	12	19	26	..
TU	.	6	13	20	27	..
W	.	7	A	21	28	..
TH	1	8	15	22	29	..
F	PR	9	16	23	..	..
Sa	3	10	17	24	..	..

MARCH

Su	.	L^3	L^4	L^5	P	E
M	.	4	11	18	25	..
TU	.	5	12	19	26	..
W	.	6	13	20	27	..
TH	.	7	14	21	M	..
F	1	8	15	22	G	..
Sa	2	9	16	23	30	..

APRIL

Su	.	E^2	E^3	E^4	E^5	..
M	1	An	15	22	29	..
TU	2	9	16	23	30	..
W	3	10	17	24	..	..
TH	4	11	18	25	..	..
F	5	12	19	26	..	..
Sa	6	13	20	27	..	..

MAY

Su	.	E^6	E^7	W	T	..
M	.	6	13	20	27	..
TU	.	7	14	21	28	..
W	1	8	15	22	29	..
TH	2	A	16	23	30	..
F	3	10	17	24	31	..
Sa	4	11	18	25	..	..

JUNE

Su	.	T^1	T^2	T^3	T^4	T^5
M	.	3	10	17	24	..
TU	.	4	11	18	25	..
W	.	5	12	19	26	..
TH	.	6	13	20	27	..
F	.	7	14	21	28	..
Sa	1	8	15	22	29	..

The Calendars for 2024 and 2025 follow *The New Lectionary and Calendar*

Key to calendar notes (continued on pages 5 and 6)

A = Ash Wednesday, Ascension, Advent
A^- = Before Advent
A^{-4} = also All Saints, 2024 and 2025 (if transferred)
A^{-1} = Christ the King
An = Annunciation
AS = All Saints
B = Baptism

Calendar 2024

JULY						
Su	.	T^{6}	T^{7}	T^{8}	T^{9}	..
M	1	8	15	22	29	..
TU	2	9	16	23	30	..
W	3	10	17	24	31	..
TH	4	11	18	25	..	..
F	5	12	19	26	..	..
Sa	6	13	20	27	..	..

AUGUST						
Su	.	T^{10}	T^{11}	T^{12}	T^{13}	..
M	.	5	12	19	26	..
TU	.	6	13	20	27	..
W	.	7	14	21	28	..
TH	1	8	15	22	29	..
F	2	9	16	23	30	..
Sa	3	10	17	24	31	..

SEPTEMBER						
Su	T^{14}	T^{15}	T^{16}	T^{17}	T^{18}	..
M	2	9	16	23	30	..
TU	3	10	17	24	..	..
W	4	11	18	25	..	..
TH	5	12	19	26	..	..
F	6	13	20	27	..	..
Sa	7	14	21	28	..	..

OCTOBER						
Su	.	T^{19}	T^{20}	T^{21}	T^{L}	..
M	.	7	14	21	28	..
TU	1	8	15	22	29	..
W	2	9	16	23	30	..
TH	3	10	17	24	31	..
F	4	11	18	25	..	..
Sa	5	12	19	26	..	..

NOVEMBER						
Su	.	A^{-4}	A^{-3}	A^{-2}	A^{-1}	..
M	.	4	11	18	25	..
TU	.	5	12	19	26	..
W	.	6	13	20	27	..
TH	.	7	14	21	28	..
F	AS	8	15	22	29	..
Sa	2	9	16	23	30	..

DECEMBER						
Su	A^{1}	A^{2}	A^{3}	A^{4}	X^{1}	..
M	2	9	16	23	30	..
TU	3	10	17	24	31	..
W	4	11	18	X	..	..
TH	5	12	19	26	..	..
F	6	13	20	27	..	..
Sa	7	14	21	28	..	..

E = Epiphany, Easter
E^{4} = also Presentation, 2024 (if transferred)
G = Good Friday
L = Lent
L^{-} = Before Lent
M = Maundy Thursday

Calendar 2025

JANUARY

Su	.	X^2	B	E^2	E^3	..
M	.	E	13	20	27	..
TU	.	7	14	21	28	..
W	1	8	15	22	29	..
TH	2	9	16	23	30	..
F	3	10	17	24	31	..
Sa	4	11	18	25	..	..

FEBRUARY

Su	.	Pr	L^{-4}	L^{-3}	L^{-2}	..
M	.	3	10	17	24	..
TU	.	4	11	18	25	..
W	.	5	12	19	26	..
TH	.	6	13	20	27	..
F	.	7	14	21	28	..
Sa	1	8	15	22	..	..

MARCH

Su	.	L^{-1}	L^1	L^2	L^3	L^4
M	.	3	10	17	24	31
TU	.	4	11	18	An	..
W	.	A	12	19	26	..
TH	.	6	13	20	27	..
F	.	7	14	21	28	..
Sa	1	8	15	22	29	..

APRIL

Su	.	L^5	P	E	E^2	..
M	.	7	14	21	28	..
TU	1	8	15	22	29	..
W	2	9	16	23	30	..
TH	3	10	M	24	..	..
F	4	11	F	25	..	..
Sa	5	12	19	26	..	..

MAY

Su	.	E^3	E^4	E^5	E^6	..
M	.	5	12	19	26	..
TU	.	6	13	20	27	..
W	.	7	14	21	28	..
TH	1	8	15	22	A	..
F	2	9	16	23	30	..
Sa	3	10	17	24	31	..

JUNE

Su	E^7	W	T	T^1	T^2	..
M	2	9	16	23	30	..
TU	3	10	17	24	..	..
W	4	11	18	25	..	..
TH	5	12	19	26	..	..
F	6	13	20	27	..	..
Sa	7	14	21	28	..	..

P = Palm Sunday
Pr = Presentation
T = Trinity
(T^2 = also Peter and Paul, 2025)
(T^{13} = also Holy Cross Day, 2025)
(T^{14} = also Matthew, 2025)
(T^{18} = also Michael and All Angels, 2024)
T^L = Last Sunday after Trinity
W = Pentecost (Whit Sunday)
X = Christmas

Calendar 2025

JULY						
Su	.	T^{3}	T^{4}	T^{5}	T^{6}	..
M	.	7	14	21	28	..
TU	1	8	15	22	29	..
W	2	9	16	23	30	..
TH	3	10	17	24	31	..
F	4	11	18	25	..	..
Sa	5	12	19	26	..	..

AUGUST						
Su	.	T^{7}	T^{8}	T^{9}	T^{10}	T^{11}
M	.	4	11	18	25	..
TU	.	5	12	19	26	..
W	.	6	13	20	27	..
TH	.	7	14	21	28	..
F	1	8	15	22	29	..
Sa	2	9	16	23	30	..

SEPTEMBER						
Su	.	T^{12}	T^{13}	T^{14}	T^{15}	..
M	1	8	15	22	29	..
TU	2	9	16	23	30	..
W	3	10	17	24	..	..
TH	4	11	18	25	..	..
F	5	12	19	26	..	..
Sa	6	13	20	27	..	..

OCTOBER						
Su	.	T^{16}	T^{17}	T^{18}	T^{L}	..
M	.	6	13	20	27	..
TU	.	7	14	21	28	..
W	1	8	15	22	29	..
TH	2	9	16	23	30	..
F	3	10	17	24	31	..
Sa	4	11	18	25	..	..

NOVEMBER						
Su	.	A^{-4}	A^{-3}	A^{-2}	A^{-1}	A
M	.	3	10	17	24	..
TU	.	4	11	18	25	..
W	.	5	12	19	26	..
TH	.	6	13	20	27	..
F	.	7	14	21	28	..
Sa	AS	8	15	22	29	..

DECEMBER						
Su	.	A^{2}	A^{3}	A^{4}	X^{1}	..
M	1	8	15	22	29	..
TU	2	9	16	23	30	..
W	3	10	17	24	31	..
TH	4	11	18	X	..	..
F	5	12	19	26	..	..
Sa	6	13	20	27	..	..

MOVEABLE FEASTS 2023–2033

Year	Ash Wednesday	Easter Day	Ascension Day	Pentecost Whit Sunday	First Sunday of Advent	Christmas Day
2023	Feb 22	Apr 9	May 18	May 28	Dec 3	Mon
2024	Feb 14	Mar 31	May 9	May 19	Dec 1	Wed
2025	Mar 5	Apr 20	May 29	June 8	Nov 30	Thu
2026	Feb 18	Apr 5	May 14	May 24	Nov 29	Fri
2027	Feb 10	Mar 28	May 6	May 16	Nov 28	Sat
2028	Mar 1	Apr 16	May 25	June 4	Dec 3	Mon
2029	Feb 14	Apr 1	May 10	May 20	Dec 2	Tue
2030	Mar 6	Apr 21	May 30	June 9	Dec 1	Wed
2031	Feb 26	Apr 13	May 22	June 1	Nov 30	Thu
2032	Feb 11	Mar 28	May 6	May 16	Nov 28	Sat
2033	Mar 2	Apr 17	May 26	June 5	Nov 27	Sun

Notes to the diary pages

In the following diary pages, names of Sundays (in **bold** type) are in accordance with *The Common Worship Calendar and Lectionary*, with the titles preferred by The Book of Common Prayer (in *italic* type) being listed beneath them. Festivals (in **bold** type) are distinguished by *CW* and BCP when the calendars diverge, and when the rules require a Festival to be transferred, the alternative date is shown. Principal Feasts and other Principal Holy Days are in **BOLD CAPITALS**. Other days and traditional titles are in ordinary type. For *The Common Worship Calendar and Lectionary* applied to December 2023 and in full to the year 2024, see the Lectionary on pages 134–276.

Astronomical and Calendarial information is reproduced with permission. © Crown Copyright and/or database rights. Reproduced by permission of the Controller of Her Majesty's Stationery Office and the UK Hydrographic Office (*www.gov.uk/ukho*).

Certain dates are subject to change and regional variation.

December 2023

3 Sunday **The First Sunday of Advent**
1 in Advent

4 Monday

5 Tuesday

Wednesday **6**

Thursday **7**

Friday **8**

Saturday **9**

December 2023

10 Sunday **The Second Sunday of Advent**
2 in Advent

11 Monday

12 Tuesday

Ember Day (*CW* and BCP) Wednesday **13**

Thursday **14**

Ember Day (*CW* and BCP) Friday **15**

Ember Day (*CW* and BCP) Saturday **16**

December 2023

17 Sunday

The Third Sunday of Advent
3 in Advent

18 Monday

19 Tuesday

Wednesday **20**

Thomas the Apostle (BCP)
(*CW* 3 July)

Thursday **21**

Friday **22**

Saturday **23**

December 2023

24 Sunday

The Fourth Sunday of Advent
4 in Advent
Christmas Eve

25 Monday

CHRISTMAS DAY
Bank Holiday (England, N. Ireland, Scotland, Wales and Rep. of Ireland)

26 Tuesday

Stephen, Deacon, First Martyr
Bank Holiday (England, N. Ireland, Scotland, Wales and Rep. of Ireland)

John, Apostle and Evangelist Wednesday **27**

The Holy Innocents Thursday **28**

Friday **29**

Saturday **30**

Dec 2023/Jan 2024

31 Sunday

The First Sunday of Christmas
Sunday after Christmas Day

1 Monday

The Naming and Circumcision of Jesus (*CW*)
The Circumcision of Christ (BCP)
Bank Holiday (England, N. Ireland, Scotland, Wales and Rep. of Ireland)

2 Tuesday

Bank Holiday (Scotland)

Wednesday **3**

Thursday **4**

Friday **5**

THE EPIPHANY Saturday **6**

7 Sunday

The Baptism of Christ
1 after Epiphany

8 Monday

9 Tuesday

Wednesday **10**

Thursday **11**

Friday **12**

Saturday **13**

January 2024

14 Sunday **The Second Sunday of Epiphany**
2 after Epiphany

15 Monday

16 Tuesday

Wednesday **17**

The Week of Prayer for Christian Unity until 25th

Thursday **18**

Friday **19**

Saturday **20**

January 2024

21 Sunday **The Third Sunday of Epiphany**
3 after Epiphany

22 Monday

23 Tuesday

Wednesday **24**

The Conversion of Paul Thursday **25**

Friday **26**

Saturday **27**

January 2024

28 Sunday **The Fourth Sunday of Epiphany**
Septuagesima

29 Monday

30 Tuesday

Wednesday **31**

Thursday **1**

THE PRESENTATION OF CHRIST IN THE TEMPLE (CANDLEMAS)

Friday **2**

Saturday **3**

February 2024

4 Sunday **The Second Sunday before Lent**
Sexagesima

5 Monday

6 Tuesday

Wednesday **7**

Thursday **8**

Friday **9**

Saturday **10**

February 2024

11 Sunday

The Sunday next before Lent
Quinquagesima

12 Monday

13 Tuesday

ASH WEDNESDAY Wednesday **14**

Thomas Bray, founder of SPCK (died 1730) Thursday **15**

Friday **16**

Saturday **17**

18 Sunday

The First Sunday of Lent
1 in Lent

19 Monday

20 Tuesday

Ember Day
(*CW* and BCP)

Wednesday **21**

Thursday **22**

Ember Day
(*CW* and BCP)

Friday **23**

Matthias the Apostle (BCP)
(*CW* 14 May)
Ember Day
(*CW* and BCP)

Saturday **24**

25 Sunday **The Second Sunday of Lent**
2 in Lent

26 Monday

27 Tuesday

Wednesday **28**

Thursday **29**

David, Bishop,
Patron of Wales

Friday **1**

Saturday **2**

3 Sunday **The Third Sunday of Lent**
3 in Lent

4 Monday

5 Tuesday

Wednesday **6**

Thursday **7**

Friday **8**

Saturday **9**

March 2024

10 Sunday

The Fourth Sunday of Lent
4 in Lent
Mothering Sunday

11 Monday

12 Tuesday

Wednesday **13**

Thursday **14**

Friday **15**

Saturday **16**

March 2024

17 Sunday

The Fifth Sunday of Lent
5 in Lent
Patrick, Bishop, Missionary, Patron of Ireland

18 Monday

Bank Holiday
(N. Ireland and Rep. of Ireland)

19 Tuesday

Joseph of Nazareth (*CW*)

Wednesday **20**

Thursday **21**

Friday **22**

Saturday **23**

24 Sunday **Palm Sunday**

25 Monday

26 Tuesday

Wednesday **27**

MAUNDY THURSDAY Thursday **28**

GOOD FRIDAY Friday **29**
Bank Holiday (England,
N. Ireland, Scotland and Wales)

Easter Eve Saturday **30**
Summer Time
begins tomorrow

March/April 2024

31 Sunday **EASTER DAY**

1 Monday Bank Holiday (England, N. Ireland, Wales and Rep. of Ireland)

2 Tuesday

Wednesday **3**

Thursday **4**

Friday **5**

Saturday **6**

April 2024

7 Sunday **The Second Sunday of Easter**
1 after Easter

8 Monday **THE ANNUNCIATION OF OUR LORD TO THE BLESSED VIRGIN MARY**

9 Tuesday

Wednesday **10**

Thursday **11**

Friday **12**

Saturday **13**

14 Sunday

The Third Sunday of Easter
2 after Easter

15 Monday

16 Tuesday

Wednesday **17**

Thursday **18**

Friday **19**

Saturday **20**

April 2024

21 Sunday

The Fourth Sunday of Easter
3 after Easter

22 Monday

23 Tuesday

George, Martyr, Patron of England

Wednesday **24**

Mark the Evangelist Thursday **25**

Friday **26**

Saturday **27**

28 Sunday **The Fifth Sunday of Easter**
4 after Easter

29 Monday **Philip and James, Apostles**

30 Tuesday

Philip and James, Apostles Wednesday **1**

Thursday **2**

Friday **3**

Saturday **4**

5 Sunday

The Sixth Sunday of Easter
5 after Easter

6 Monday

Rogation Day
Bank Holiday (England, N. Ireland, Scotland, Wales and Rep. of Ireland)

7 Tuesday

Rogation Day

Rogation Day

Wednesday **8**

ASCENSION DAY

Thursday **9**

Friday **10**

Saturday **11**

12 Sunday **The Seventh Sunday of Easter**
6 after Easter

13 Monday

14 Tuesday **Matthias the Apostle** (*CW*)
(BCP 24 February)

Wednesday **15**

Thursday **16**

Friday **17**

Saturday **18**

19 Sunday

DAY OF PENTECOST
WHIT SUNDAY

20 Monday

21 Tuesday

Ember Day (BCP) Wednesday **22**

Thursday **23**

Ember Day (BCP) Friday **24**

Ember Day (BCP) Saturday **25**

26 Sunday **TRINITY SUNDAY**

27 Monday Bank Holiday (England, N. Ireland, Scotland and Wales)

28 Tuesday

Wednesday **29**

Day of Thanksgiving for Holy Communion (Corpus Christi) (*CW*)

Thursday **30**

The Visit of the Blessed Virgin Mary to Elizabeth (*CW*)

Friday **31**

Saturday **1**

2 Sunday

The First Sunday after Trinity
1 after Trinity

3 Monday

Bank Holiday
(Rep. of Ireland)

4 Tuesday

Wednesday **5**

Thursday **6**

Friday **7**

Saturday **8**

June 2024

9 Sunday **The Second Sunday after Trinity**

2 after Trinity

10 Monday

11 Tuesday **Barnabas the Apostle**

Wednesday **12**

Thursday **13**

Friday **14**

Saturday **15**

June 2024

16 Sunday **The Third Sunday after Trinity**

3 after Trinity

17 Monday

18 Tuesday

Wednesday **19**

Thursday **20**

Friday **21**

Saturday **22**

23 Sunday **The Fourth Sunday after Trinity**
4 after Trinity

24 Monday **The Birth of John the Baptist**

25 Tuesday

Ember Day (*CW*)

Wednesday **26**

Thursday **27**

Ember Day (*CW*)

Friday **28**

Peter and Paul, Apostles (*CW*)
Peter the Apostle (BCP)
Ember Day (*CW*)

Saturday **29**

30 Sunday

The Fifth Sunday after Trinity
5 after Trinity

1 Monday

2 Tuesday

Wednesday **3**

Thomas the Apostle (*CW*)
(BCP 21 December)

Thursday **4**

Friday **5**

Saturday **6**

7 Sunday

The Sixth Sunday after Trinity

6 after Trinity

8 Monday

9 Tuesday

Wednesday **10**

Thursday **11**

Bank Holiday
(N. Ireland)

Friday **12**

Saturday **13**

July 2024

14 Sunday **The Seventh Sunday after Trinity**
7 after Trinity

15 Monday

16 Tuesday

Wednesday **17**

Thursday **18**

Friday **19**

Saturday **20**

July 2024

21 Sunday **The Eighth Sunday after Trinity**
8 after Trinity

22 Monday **Mary Magdalene**

23 Tuesday

Wednesday **24**

James the Apostle

Thursday **25**

Friday **26**

Saturday **27**

July 2024

28 Sunday **The Ninth Sunday after Trinity**

9 after Trinity

29 Monday

30 Tuesday

Wednesday **31**

Thursday **1**

Friday **2**

Saturday **3**

August 2024

4 Sunday **The Tenth Sunday after Trinity**
10 after Trinity

5 Monday Bank Holiday
(Scotland and Rep. of Ireland)

6 Tuesday **The Transfiguration of Our Lord**

Wednesday **7**

Thursday **8**

Friday **9**

Saturday **10**

August 2024

11 Sunday **The Eleventh Sunday after Trinity**
11 after Trinity

12 Monday

13 Tuesday

Wednesday **14**

The Blessed Virgin Mary (*CW*)

Thursday **15**

Friday **16**

Saturday **17**

18 Sunday **The Twelfth Sunday after Trinity**
12 after Trinity

19 Monday

20 Tuesday

Wednesday **21**

Thursday **22**

Friday **23**

Bartholomew the Apostle Saturday **24**

August 2024

25 Sunday **The Thirteenth Sunday after Trinity**
13 after Trinity

26 Monday Bank Holiday (England, N. Ireland and Wales)

27 Tuesday

Wednesday **28**

Thursday **29**

Friday **30**

Saturday **31**

September 2024

1 Sunday **The Fourteenth Sunday after Trinity**

14 after Trinity

2 Monday

3 Tuesday

Wednesday **4**

Thursday **5**

Friday **6**

Saturday **7**

September 2024

8 Sunday

The Fifteenth Sunday after Trinity
15 after Trinity
Education Sunday
The King's Accession (in 2022)

9 Monday

10 Tuesday

Wednesday **11**

Thursday **12**

Friday **13**

Holy Cross Day Saturday **14**

September 2024

15 Sunday **The Sixteenth Sunday after Trinity**

16 after Trinity

16 Monday

17 Tuesday

Ember Day (BCP)

Wednesday **18**

Thursday **19**

Ember Day (BCP)

Friday **20**

Matthew,
Apostle and Evangelist
Ember Day (BCP)

Saturday **21**

September 2024

22 Sunday **The Seventeenth Sunday after Trinity**

17 after Trinity

23 Monday

24 Tuesday

Ember Day (*CW*)

Wednesday **25**

Thursday **26**

Michael and All Angels
Ember Day (*CW*)

Friday **27**

Ember Day (*CW*)

Saturday **28**

Sept/Oct 2024

29 Sunday **The Eighteenth Sunday after Trinity**
18 after Trinity
Michael and All Angels

30 Monday

1 Tuesday

Wednesday **2**

Thursday **3**

Friday **4**

Saturday **5**

October 2024

6 Sunday **The Nineteenth Sunday after Trinity**
19 after Trinity

7 Monday

8 Tuesday

Wednesday **9**

Thursday **10**

Friday **11**

Saturday **12**

October 2024

13 Sunday **The Twentieth Sunday after Trinity**
20 after Trinity

14 Monday

15 Tuesday

Wednesday **16**

Thursday **17**

Luke the Evangelist

Friday **18**

Saturday **19**

October 2024

20 Sunday **The Twenty-first Sunday after Trinity**

21 after Trinity

21 Monday

22 Tuesday

Wednesday **23**

Thursday **24**

Friday **25**

Summer Time
ends tomorrow

Saturday **26**

27 Sunday

The Last Sunday after Trinity
22 after Trinity
Bible Sunday
Summer Time ends

28 Monday

Simon and Jude, Apostles
Bank Holiday (Rep. of Ireland)

29 Tuesday

Wednesday **30**

Thursday **31**

ALL SAINTS' DAY

Friday **1**

Saturday **2**

November 2024

3 Sunday

The Fourth Sunday before Advent

23 after Trinity

4 Monday

5 Tuesday

Wednesday **6**

Thursday **7**

Friday **8**

Saturday **9**

November 2024

10 Sunday

The Third Sunday before Advent
24 after Trinity
Remembrance Sunday

11 Monday

12 Tuesday

Wednesday **13**

Thursday **14**

Friday **15**

Saturday **16**

17 Sunday **The Second Sunday before Advent**
25 after Trinity

18 Monday

19 Tuesday

Wednesday **20**

Thursday **21**

Friday **22**

Saturday **23**

November 2024

24 Sunday

Christ the King
Sunday next before Advent

25 Monday

26 Tuesday

Wednesday **27**

Thursday **28**

Friday **29**

Andrew the Apostle Saturday **30**

December 2024

1 Sunday **The First Sunday of Advent**

1 in Advent

2 Monday Bank Holiday (Scotland)

3 Tuesday

Wednesday **4**

Thursday **5**

Friday **6**

Saturday **7**

December 2024

8 Sunday **The Second Sunday of Advent**
2 in Advent

9 Monday

10 Tuesday

Ember Day (*CW*) Wednesday **11**

Thursday **12**

Ember Day (*CW*) Friday **13**

Ember Day (*CW*) Saturday **14**

December 2024

15 Sunday **The Third Sunday of Advent**
3 in Advent

16 Monday

17 Tuesday

Ember Day (BCP) | Wednesday **18**

Thursday **19**

Ember Day (BCP) | Friday **20**

Thomas the Apostle (BCP)
(*CW* 3 July)
Ember Day (BCP) | Saturday **21**

December 2024

22 Sunday **The Fourth Sunday of Advent**
4 in Advent

23 Monday

24 Tuesday Christmas Eve

CHRISTMAS DAY
Bank Holiday (England, N. Ireland, Scotland, Wales and Rep. of Ireland)

Wednesday **25**

Stephen, Deacon, First Martyr
Bank Holiday (England, N. Ireland, Scotland, Wales and Rep. of Ireland)

Thursday **26**

John, Apostle and Evangelist

Friday **27**

The Holy Innocents

Saturday **28**

December 2024

29 Sunday

The First Sunday of Christmas
Sunday after Christmas Day

30 Monday

31 Tuesday

January 2025

Wednesday 1

The Naming and Circumcision of Jesus (*CW*)
The Circumcision of Christ (BCP)
Bank Holiday (England, N. Ireland, Scotland, Wales and Rep. of Ireland)

Thursday 2

Bank Holiday (Scotland)

Friday 3

Saturday 4

January 2025

5 Sunday **The Second Sunday of Christmas**
2 after Christmas

6 Monday **THE EPIPHANY**

7 Tuesday

Reminders for 2025

January

February

Reminders for 2025

March

April

Reminders for 2025

May

June

Reminders for 2025

July

August

Reminders for 2025

September

October

Reminders for 2025

November

December

Memoranda

Notes on the Lectionary

Making choices in *Common Worship*

Common Worship makes provision for a variety of pastoral and liturgical circumstances. It needs to, for it has to serve some church communities where Morning Prayer, Holy Communion and Evening Prayer are all celebrated every day, and yet be useful also in a church with only one service a week, and that service varying in form and time from week to week.

At the beginning of the year, some decisions in principle need to be taken.

In relation to the Calendar, whether to keep The Epiphany on Saturday 6 January or on Sunday 7 January, whether to keep The Presentation of Christ (Candlemas) on Friday 2 February or on Sunday 28 January, and whether to keep the Feast of All Saints on Friday 1 November or on Sunday 3 November.

In relation to the Lectionary

The initial choices every year to decide in relation to Sundays are:

- which of the services on a Principal Feast, Principal Holy Day, Sunday or Festival constitutes the 'Principal Service'; then use the Principal Service Lectionary (column 3) consistently for that service through the year;
- during the Sundays after Trinity, whether to use Track I of the Principal Service Lectionary (column 2), where the first reading stays over several weeks with one Old Testament book read semi-continuously, or Track 2 (column 3), where the first reading is chosen for its relationship to the Gospel reading of the day;
- which, if any, service on a Principal Feast, Principal Holy Day, Sunday or Festival constitutes the 'Second Service'; then use the Second Service Lectionary (column 5) consistently for that service through the year;
- which, if any, service on a Principal Feast, Principal Holy Day, Sunday or Festival constitutes the 'Third Service'; then use the Third Service Lectionary (column 4) consistently for that service through the year.

In relation to weekdays

- whether to use the Daily Eucharistic Lectionary (column 3) consistently for weekday celebrations of Holy Communion (with the exception of Principal Feasts, Principal Holy Days and Festivals) or to make some use of the Lesser Festival provision;
- whether to follow the first psalm provision in column 4 (morning) and column 5 (evening), where psalms during the seasons have a seasonal flavour but in ordinary time follow a sequential pattern; or to follow the alternative provision in the same columns, where psalms follow the sequential pattern throughout the year, except for the period between 19 December and The Epiphany and from the Monday of Holy Week to the Saturday of Easter Week; or to follow the psalm cycle in the Book of Common Prayer, where they are nearly always used 'in course'.

The flexibility of *Common Worship* is intended to enable the church and the minister to find the most helpful provision for them. But once a decision is made, it is advisable to stay with that decision through the year or at the very least through a complete season.

December 2023		Sunday Principal Service Weekday Eucharist	Third Service Morning Prayer	Second Service Evening Prayer
3 Sunday	**THE FIRST SUNDAY OF ADVENT** *Common Worship* Year B begins			
P		Isa. 64. 1–9 Ps. 80. 1–8, 18–20 (*or* 80. 1–8) 1 Cor. 1. 3–9 Mark 13. 24–end	Ps. 44 Isa. 2. 1–5 Luke 12. 35–48	Ps. 25 (*or* 25. 1–9) Isa. 1. 1–20 Matt. 21. 1–13
4 Monday	*John of Damascus, Monk, Teacher, c. 749; Nicholas Ferrar, Deacon, Founder of the Little Gidding Community, 1637* Daily Eucharistic Lectionary Year 2 begins			
P		Isa. 2. 1–5 Ps. 122 Matt. 8. 5–11	Ps. ***50***; 54 *alt.* Ps. ***1***; 2; 3 Isa. 25. 1–9 Matt. 12. 1–21	Ps. 70; ***71*** *alt.* Ps. ***4***; 7 Isa. 42. 18–end Rev. ch. 19
5 Tuesday				
P		Isa. 11. 1–10 Ps. 72. 1–4, 18–19 Luke 10. 21–24	Ps. ***80***; 82 *alt.* Ps. ***5***; 6; (8) Isa. 26. 1–13 Matt. 12. 22–37	Ps. ***74***; 75 *alt.* Ps. ***9***; 10† Isa. 43. 1–13 Rev. ch. 20

6 Wednesday **Nicholas, Bishop of Myra, c. 326**

Pw	Com. Bishop *also* Isa. 61. 1–3 1 Tim. 6. 6–11 Mark 10. 13–16	*or*	Isa. 25. 6–10a Ps. 23 Matt. 15. 29–37	Ps. 5; ***7*** *alt.* Ps. 119. 1–32 Isa. 28. 1–13 Matt. 12. 38–end	Ps. 76; ***77*** *alt.* Ps. ***11***; 12; 13 Isa. 43. 14–end Rev. 21. 1–8

7 Thursday **Ambrose, Bishop of Milan, Teacher, 397**

Pw	Com. Teacher *also* Isa. 41. 9b–13 Luke 22. 24–30	*or*	Isa. 26. 1–6 Ps. 118. 18–27a Matt. 7. 21, 24–27	Ps. ***42***; 43 *alt.* Ps. 14; ***15***; 16 Isa. 28. 14–end Matt. 13. 1–23	Ps. ***40***; 46 *alt.* Ps. 18† Isa. 44. 1–8 Rev. 21. 9–21

8 Friday **The Conception of the Blessed Virgin Mary**

Pw	Com. BVM	*or*	Isa. 29. 17–end Ps. 27. 1–4, 16–17 Matt. 9. 27–31	Ps. ***25***; 26 *alt.* Ps. 17; ***19*** Isa. 29. 1–14 Matt. 13. 24–43	Ps. 16; ***17*** *alt.* Ps. 22 Isa. 44. 9–23 Rev. 21.22 – 22.5

December 2023		Sunday Principal Service Weekday Eucharist	Third Service Morning Prayer	Second Service Evening Prayer
9 Saturday				
P		Isa. 30. 19–21, 23–26 Ps. 146. 4–9 Matt. 9.35 – 10.1, 6–8	Ps. ***9***; 10 *alt.* Ps. 20; 21; ***23*** Isa. 29. 15–end Matt. 13. 44–end	Ps. ***27***; 28 *alt.* Ps. ***24***; 25 Isa. 44.24 – 45.13 Rev. 22. 6–end **ct**
10 Sunday	**THE SECOND SUNDAY OF ADVENT**			
P		Isa. 40. 1–11 Ps. 85. 1–2, 8–end (*or* 85. 8–end) 2 Pet. 3. 8–15a Mark 1. 1–8	Ps. 80 Baruch 5. 1–9 *or* Zeph. 3. 14–end Luke 1. 5–20	Ps. 40 (*or* 40. 12–end) 1 Kings 22. 1–28 Rom. 15. 4–13 *Gospel*: Matt. 11. 2–11
11 Monday				
P		Isa. ch. 35 Ps. 85. 7–end Luke 5. 17–26	Ps. 44 *alt.* Ps. 27; ***30*** Isa. 30. 1–18 Matt. 14. 1–12	Ps. ***144***; 146 *alt.* Ps. 26; ***28***; 29 Isa. 45. 14–end 1 Thess. ch. 1

12 Tuesday					
P			Isa. 40. 1-11 Ps. 96. 1, 10-end Matt. 18. 12-14	Ps. ***56***; 57 *alt*. Ps. 32; ***36*** Isa. 30. 19-end Matt. 14. 13-end	Ps. ***11***; 12; 13 *alt*. Ps. 33 Isa. ch. 46 1 Thess. 2. 1-12
13 Wednesday	**Lucy, Martyr at Syracuse, 304** Ember Day *Samuel Johnson, Moralist, 1784*				
Pr	Com. Martyr *also* Wisd. 3. 1-7 2 Cor. 4. 6-15	*or*	Isa. 40. 25-end Ps. 103. 8-13 Matt. 11. 28-end	Ps. ***62***; 63 *alt*. Ps. 34 Isa. ch. 31 Matt. 15. 1-20	Ps. ***10***; 14 *alt*. Ps. 119. 33-56 Isa. ch. 47 1 Thess. 2. 13-end
14 Thursday	**John of the Cross, Poet, Teacher, 1591**				
Pw	Com. Teacher *esp*. 1 Cor. 2. 1-10 *also* John 14. 18-23	*or*	Isa. 41. 13-20 Ps. 145. 1, 8-13 Matt. 11. 11-15	Ps. 53; ***54***; 60 *alt*. Ps. 37† Isa. ch. 32 Matt. 15. 21-28	Ps. 73 *alt*. Ps. 39; ***40*** Isa. 48. 1-11 1 Thess. ch. 3

December 2023		Sunday Principal Service Weekday Eucharist	Third Service Morning Prayer	Second Service Evening Prayer
15 Friday	Ember Day			
P		Isa. 48. 17–19 Ps. 1 Matt. 11. 16–19	Ps. 85; ***86*** *alt.* Ps. 31 Isa. 33. 1–22 Matt. 15. 29–end	Ps. 82; ***90*** *alt.* Ps. 35 Isa. 48. 12–end 1 Thess. 4. 1–12
16 Saturday	Ember Day			
P		Ecclus. 48. 1–4, 9–11 *or* 2 Kings 2. 9–12 Ps. 80. 1–4, 18–19 Matt. 17. 10–13	Ps. 145 *alt.* Ps. 41; ***42***; 43 Isa. ch. 35 Matt. 16. 1–12	Ps. 93; ***94*** *alt.* Ps. 45; ***46*** Isa. 49. 1–13 1 Thess. 4. 13–end **ct**
17 Sunday	**THE THIRD SUNDAY OF ADVENT** O Sapientia*			
P		Isa. 61. 1–4, 8–end Ps. 126 *or Canticle*: Magnificat 1 Thess. 5. 16–24 John 1. 6–8, 19–28	Ps. 50. 1–6; 62 Isa. ch. 12 Luke 1. 57–66	Ps. 68. 1–19 (*or* 68. 1–8) Mal. 3. 1–4; ch. 4 Phil. 4. 4–7 *Gospel*: Matt. 14. 1–12

18 Monday

P	Jer. 23. 5–8 Ps. 72. 1–2, 12–13, 18–end Matt. 1. 18–24	Ps. 40 *alt*. Ps. 44 Isa. 38. 1–8, 21–22 Matt. 16. 13–end	Ps. 25; ***26*** *alt*. Ps. ***47***; 49 Isa. 49. 14–25 1 Thess. 5. 1–11

19 Tuesday

P	Judg. 13. 2–7, 24–end Ps. 71. 3–8 Luke 1. 5–25	Ps. 144; ***146*** Isa. 38. 9–20 Matt. 17. 1–13	Ps. 10; ***57*** Isa. ch. 50 1 Thess. 5. 12–end

20 Wednesday

P	Isa. 7. 10–14 Ps. 24. 1–6 Luke 1. 26–38	Ps. ***46***; 95 Isa. ch. 39 Matt. 17. 14–21	Ps. ***4***; 9 Isa. 51. 1–8 2 Thess. ch. 1

21 Thursday**

P	Zeph. 3. 14–18 Ps. 33. 1–4, 11–12, 20–end Luke 1. 39–45	Ps. ***121***; 122; 123 Zeph. 1.1 – 2.3 Matt. 17. 22–end	Ps. 80; ***84*** Isa. 51. 9–16 2 Thess. ch. 2

*Evening Prayer readings from the Additional Weekday Lectionary may be used from 17 to 23 December.
**Thomas the Apostle may be celebrated on 21 December instead of 3 July.

December 2023		Sunday Principal Service Weekday Eucharist	Third Service Morning Prayer	Second Service Evening Prayer
22 Friday				
P		1 Sam. 1. 24–end Ps. 113 Luke 1. 46–56	Ps. ***124***; 125; 126; 127 Zeph. 3. 1–13 Matt. 18. 1–20	Ps. 24; ***48*** Isa. 51. 17–end 2 Thess. ch. 3
23 Saturday				
P		Mal. 3. 1–4; 4. 5–end Ps. 25. 3–9 Luke 1. 57–66	Ps. 128; 129; ***130***; 131 Zeph. 3. 14–end Matt. 18. 21–end	Ps. 89. 1–37 Isa. 52. 1–12 Jude **ct**
24 Sunday	**THE FOURTH SUNDAY OF ADVENT CHRISTMAS EVE**			
P		2 Sam. 7. 1–11, 16 *Canticle*: Magnificat *or* Ps. 89. 1–4, 19–26 (*or* 1–8) Rom. 16. 25–end Luke 1. 26–38	Ps. 144 Isa. 7. 10–16 Rom. 1. 1–7	*Evening Prayer* Ps. 85 Zech. ch. 2 Rev. 1. 1–8

25 Monday **CHRISTMAS DAY**

𝔚

Any of the following sets of readings may be used on the evening of Christmas Eve and on Christmas Day. Set III should be used at some service during the celebration.

I
Isa. 9. 2–7
Ps. 96
Titus 2. 11–14
Luke 2. 1–14 [15–20]

II
Isa. 62. 6–end
Ps. 97
Titus 3. 4–7
Luke 2. [1–7] 8–20

III
Isa. 52. 7–10
Ps. 98
Heb. 1. 1–4 [5–12]
John 1. 1–14

MP: Ps. ***110***; 117
Isa. 62. 1–5
Matt. 1. 18–end

EP: Ps. 8
Isa. 65. 17–25
Phil. 2. 5–11
or Luke 2. 1–20
if it has not been used at the principal service of the day

December 2023		Sunday Principal Service Weekday Eucharist	Third Service Morning Prayer	Second Service Evening Prayer
26 Tuesday	**STEPHEN, DEACON, FIRST MARTYR**			
R	*The reading from Acts must be used as either the first or second reading at the Eucharist.*	2 Chron. 24. 20–22 *or* Acts 7. 51–end Ps. 119. 161–168 Acts 7. 51–end *or* Gal. 2. 16b–20 Matt. 10. 17–22	*MP*: Ps. ***13***; 31. 1–8; 150 Jer. 26. 12–15 Acts ch. 6	*EP*: Ps. 57; ***86*** Gen. 4. 1–10 Matt. 23. 34–end
27 Wednesday	**JOHN, APOSTLE AND EVANGELIST**			
W		Exod. 33. 7–11a Ps. 117 1 John ch. 1 John 21. 19b–end	*MP*: Ps. ***21***; 147. 13–end Exod. 33. 12–end 1 John 2. 1–11	*EP*: Ps. 97 Isa. 6. 1–8 1 John 5. 1–12
28 Thursday	**THE HOLY INNOCENTS**			
R		Jer. 31. 15–17 Ps. 124 1 Cor. 1. 26–29 Matt. 2. 13–18	*MP*: Ps. ***36***; 146 Baruch 4. 21–27 *or* Gen. 37. 13–20 Matt. 18. 1–10	*EP*: Ps. 123; ***128*** Isa. 49. 14–25 Mark 10. 13–16

29 Friday	**Thomas Becket, Archbishop of Canterbury, Martyr, 1170**				
Wr	Com. Martyr *esp.* Matt. 10. 28–33 *also* Ecclus. 51. 1–8	*or*	1 John 2. 3–11 Ps. 96. 1–4 Luke 2. 22–35	Ps. ***19***; 20 Jonah ch. 1 Col. 1. 1–14	Ps. 131; ***132*** Isa. 57. 15–end John 1. 1–18
30 Saturday					
W			1 John 2. 12–17 Ps. 96. 7–10 Luke 2. 36–40	Ps. 111; 112; ***113*** Jonah ch. 2 Col. 1. 15–23	Ps. ***65***; 84 Isa. 59. 1–15a John 1. 19–28 **ct**
31 Sunday	**THE FIRST SUNDAY OF CHRISTMAS**				
W			Isa. 61.10 – 62.3 Ps. 148 (*or* 148. 7–end) Gal. 4. 4–7 Luke 2. 15–21	Ps. 105. 1–11 Isa. 63. 7–9 Eph. 3. 5–12	Ps. 132 Isa. ch. 35 Col. 1. 9–20 *or* Luke 2. 41–end *or First EP of The Naming of Jesus* Ps. 148 Jer. 23. 1–6 Col. 2. 8–15

		Sunday Principal Service Weekday Eucharist	Third Service Morning Prayer	Second Service Evening Prayer

January 2024

1 Monday	**THE NAMING AND CIRCUMCISION OF JESUS**			
W		Num. 6. 22–end Ps. 8 Gal. 4. 4–7 Luke 2. 15–21	*MP*: Ps. ***103***; 150 Gen. 17. 1–13 Rom. 2. 17–end	*EP*: Ps. 115 Deut. 30. [1–10] 11–end Acts 3. 1–16
2 Tuesday	**Basil the Great and Gregory of Nazianzus, Bishops, Teachers, 379 and 389** *Seraphim, Monk of Sarov, Spiritual Guide, 1833; Vedanayagam Samuel Azariah, Bishop in South India, Evangelist, 1945*			
W	Com. Teacher *or* *esp.* 2 Tim. 4. 1–8 Matt. 5. 13–19	1 John 2. 22–28 Ps. 98. 1–4 John 1. 19–28	Ps. 18. 1–30 Ruth ch. 1 Col. 2. 8–end	Ps. 45; ***46*** Isa. 60. 1–12 John 1. 35–42
3 Wednesday				
W		1 John 2.29 – 3.6 Ps. 98. 2–7 John 1. 29–34	Ps. ***127***; 128; 131 Ruth ch. 2 Col. 3. 1–11	Ps. ***2***; 110 Isa. 60. 13–end John 1. 43–end

4 Thursday			
W	1 John 3. 7–10 Ps. 98. 1, 8–end John 1. 35–42	Ps. 89. 1–37 Ruth ch. 3 Col. 3.12 – 4.1	Ps. 85; ***87*** Isa. ch. 61 John 2. 1–12
5 Friday			
W	1 John 3. 11–21 Ps. 100 John 1. 43–end	Ps. 8; ***48*** Ruth 4. 1–7 Col. 4. 2–end	*First EP of The Epiphany* Ps. 96; **97** Isa. 49. 1–13 John 4. 7–26 **W ct** *or, if The Epiphany is celebrated on 7 January*: Ps. 96; **97** Isa. ch. 62 John 2. 13–end

January 2024		Sunday Principal Service Weekday Eucharist	Third Service Morning Prayer	Second Service Evening Prayer
6 Saturday	**THE EPIPHANY**			
𝔚		Isa. 60. 1–6 Ps. 72. [1–9] 10–15 Eph. 3. 1–12 Matt. 2. 1–12	*MP*: Ps. ***132***; 113 Jer. 31. 7–14 John 1. 29–34	*EP*: Ps. ***98***; 100 Baruch 4.36 – 5.end *or* Isa. 60. 1–9 John 2. 1–11
	or, if The Epiphany is celebrated on 7 January:			
W		1 John 5. 5–13 Ps. 147. 13–end Mark 1. 7–11	Ps. ***99***; 147. 1–12 Baruch 1.15 – 2.10 *or* Jer. 23. 1–8 Matt. 20. 1–16	*First EP of The Epiphany* Ps. 96; 97 Isa. 49. 1–13 John 4. 7–26 **𝔚 ct**
7 Sunday	**THE BAPTISM OF CHRIST (THE FIRST SUNDAY OF EPIPHANY)** *or transferred to 8 January if The Epiphany is celebrated today. (For The Epiphany, see provision on 6 January.)*			
𝔚		Gen. 1. 1–5 Ps. 29 Acts 19. 1–7 Mark 1. 4–11	Ps. 89. 19–29 1 Sam. 16. 1–3, 13 John 1. 29–34	Ps. 46; [47] Isa. 42. 1–9 Eph. 2. 1–10 *Gospel*: Matt. 3. 13–end

8 Monday For The Baptism, see provision on 7 January.

W **DEL 1**	1 Sam. 1. 1–8 Ps. 116. 10–15 Mark 1. 14–20	Ps. ***2***; 110 *alt*. Ps. 71 Gen. 1. 1–19 Matt. 21. 1–17	Ps. ***34***; 36 *alt*. Ps. ***72***; 75 Amos ch. 1 1 Cor. 1. 1–17

9 Tuesday

W	1 Sam. 1. 9–20 *Canticle*: 1 Sam. 2. 1, 4–8 *or* Magnificat Mark 1. 21–28	Ps. 8; ***9*** *alt*. Ps. 73 Gen. 1.20 – 2.3 Matt. 21. 18–32	Ps. ***45***; 46 *alt*. Ps. 74 Amos ch. 2 1 Cor. 1. 18–end

10 Wednesday *William Laud, Archbishop of Canterbury, 1645*

W	1 Sam. 3. 1–10, 19–20 Ps. 40. 1–4, 7–10 Mark 1. 29–39	Ps. 19; ***20*** *alt*. Ps. 77 Gen. 2. 4–end Matt. 21. 33–end	Ps. ***47***; 48 *alt*. Ps. 119. 81–104 Amos ch. 3 1 Cor. ch. 2

11 Thursday *Mary Slessor, Missionary in West Africa, 1915*

W	1 Sam. 4. 1–11 Ps. 44. 10–15, 24–25 Mark 1. 40–end	Ps. ***21***; 24 *alt*. Ps. 78. 1–39† Gen. ch. 3 Matt. 22. 1–14	Ps. ***61***; 65 *alt*. Ps. 78. 40–end† Amos ch. 4 1 Cor. ch. 3

January 2024			Sunday Principal Service Weekday Eucharist	Third Service Morning Prayer	Second Service Evening Prayer
12 Friday	**Aelred of Hexham, Abbot of Rievaulx, 1167** *Benedict Biscop, Abbot of Wearmouth, Scholar, 689*				
W	Com. Religious *also* Ecclus. 15. 1–6	*or*	1 Sam. 8. 4–7, 10–end Ps. 89. 15–18 Mark 2. 1–12	Ps. ***67***; 72 *alt.* Ps. 55 Gen. 4. 1–16, 25–26 Matt. 22. 15–33	Ps. 68 *alt.* Ps. 69 Amos 5. 1–17 1 Cor. ch. 4
13 Saturday	**Hilary, Bishop of Poitiers, Teacher, 367** *Kentigern (Mungo), Missionary Bishop in Strathclyde and Cumbria, 603; George Fox, Founder of the Society of Friends (the Quakers), 1691*				
W	Com. Teacher *also* 1 John 2. 18–25 John 8. 25–32	*or*	1 Sam. 9. 1–4, 17–19; 10. 1a Ps. 21. 1–6 Mark 2. 13–17	Ps. 29; ***33*** *alt.* Ps. ***76***; 79 Gen. 6. 1–10 Matt. 22. 34–end	Ps. 84; ***85*** *alt.* Ps. 81; ***84*** Amos 5. 18–end 1 Cor. ch. 5 **ct**
14 Sunday	**THE SECOND SUNDAY OF EPIPHANY**				
W			1 Sam. 3. 1–10 [11–20] Ps. 139. 1–5, 12–18 (*or* 1–9) Rev. 5. 1–10 John 1. 43–end	Ps. 145. 1–12 Isa. 62. 1–5 1 Cor. 6. 11–end	Ps. 96 Isa. 60. 9–end Heb. 6.17 – 7.10 *Gospel*: Matt. 8. 5–13

15 Monday

W **DEL 2**			1 Sam. 15. 16–23 Ps. 50. 8–10, 16–17, 24 Mark 2. 18–22	Ps. 145; ***146*** *alt.* Ps. ***80***; 82 Gen. 6.11 – 7.10 Matt. 24. 1–14	Ps. 71 *alt.* Ps. ***85***; 86 Amos ch. 6 1 Cor. 6. 1–11

16 Tuesday

W			1 Sam. 16. 1–13 Ps. 89. 19–27 Mark 2. 23–end	Ps. ***132***; 147. 1–12 *alt.* Ps. 87; ***89. 1–18*** Gen. 7. 11–end Matt. 24. 15–28	Ps. 89. 1–37 *alt.* Ps. 89. 19–end Amos ch. 7 1 Cor. 6. 12–end

17 Wednesday **Antony of Egypt, Hermit, Abbot, 356**
Charles Gore, Bishop, Founder of the Community of the Resurrection, 1932

W	Com. Religious *esp.* Phil. 3. 7–14 *also* Matt. 19. 16–26	*or*	1 Sam. 17. 32–33, 37, 40–51 Ps. 144. 1–2, 9–10 Mark 3. 1–6	Ps. ***81***; 147. 13–end *alt.* Ps. 119. 105–128 Gen. 8. 1–14 Matt. 24. 29–end	Ps. ***97***; 98 *alt.* Ps. ***91***; 93 Amos ch. 8 1 Cor. 7. 1–24

January 2024		Sunday Principal Service Weekday Eucharist	Third Service Morning Prayer	Second Service Evening Prayer
18 Thursday	*Amy Carmichael, Founder of the Dohnavur Fellowship, Spiritual Writer, 1951* The Week of Prayer for Christian Unity until 25 January			
W		1 Sam. 18. 6–9; 19. 1–7 Ps. 56. 1–2, 8–end Mark 3. 7–12	Ps. ***76***; 148 *alt.* Ps. 90; **92** Gen. 8.15 – 9.7 Matt. 25. 1–13	Ps. 99; 100; ***111*** *alt.* Ps. 94 Amos ch. 9 1 Cor. 7. 25–end
19 Friday	**Wulfstan, Bishop of Worcester, 1095**			
W	Com. Bishop *or* *esp.* Matt. 24. 42–46	1 Sam. 24. 3–22a Ps. 57. 1–2, 8–end Mark 3. 13–19	Ps. ***27***; 149 *alt.* Ps. ***88***; (95) Gen. 9. 8–19 Matt. 25. 14–30	Ps. 73 *alt.* Ps. 102 Hos. 1.1 – 2.1 1 Cor. ch. 8
20 Saturday	*Richard Rolle of Hampole, Spiritual Writer, 1349*			
W		2 Sam. 1. 1–4, 11–12, 17–19, 23–end Ps. 80. 1–6 Mark 3. 20–21	Ps. ***122***; 128; 150 *alt.* Ps. 96; ***97***; 100 Gen. 11. 1–9 Matt. 25. 31–end	Ps. ***61***; 66 *alt.* Ps. 104 Hos. 2. 2–17 1 Cor. 9. 1–14 **ct**

21 Sunday **THE THIRD SUNDAY OF EPIPHANY**

W	Gen. 14. 17–20 Ps. 128 Rev. 19. 6–10 John 2. 1–11	Ps. 113 Jonah 3. 1–5, 10 John 3. 16–21	Ps. 33 (*or* 33. 1–12) Jer. 3.21 – 4.2 Titus 2. 1–8, 11–14 *Gospel*: Matt. 4. 12–23

22 Monday *Vincent of Saragossa, Deacon, first Martyr of Spain, 304*

W **DEL 3**	2 Sam. 5. 1–7, 10 Ps. 89. 19–27 Mark 3. 22–30	Ps. 40; ***108*** *alt*. Ps. ***98***; 99; 101 Gen. 11.27 – 12.9 Matt. 26. 1–16	Ps. ***138***; 144 *alt*. Ps. 105† (*or* Ps. 103) Hos. 2.18 – 3.end 1 Cor. 9. 15–end

23 Tuesday

W	2 Sam. 6. 12–15, 17–19 Ps. 24. 7–end Mark 3. 31–end	Ps. 34; ***36*** *alt*. Ps. 106† (*or* Ps. 103) Gen. 13. 2–end Matt. 26. 17–35	Ps. 145 *alt*. Ps. 107† Hos. 4. 1–16 1 Cor. 10. 1–13

January 2024		Sunday Principal Service Weekday Eucharist	Third Service Morning Prayer	Second Service Evening Prayer
24 Wednesday	**Francis de Sales, Bishop of Geneva, Teacher, 1622**			
W	Com. Teacher *also* Prov. 3. 13–18 John 3. 17–21	*or* 2 Sam. 7. 4–17 Ps. 89. 19–27 Mark 4. 1–20	Ps. 45; ***46*** *alt.* Ps. 110; ***111***; 112 Gen. ch. 14 Matt. 26. 36–46	Ps. 21; ***29*** *alt.* Ps. 119. 129–152 Hos. 5. 1–7 1 Cor. 10.14 – 11.1 *or First EP of The Conversion of Paul* Ps. 149 Isa. 49. 1–13 Acts 22. 3–16 **ct**
25 Thursday	**THE CONVERSION OF PAUL**			
W		Jer. 1. 4–10 *or* Acts 9. 1–22 Ps. 67 Acts 9. 1–22 *or* Gal. 1. 11–16a Matt. 19. 27–end	*MP*: Ps. 66; 147. 13–end Ezek. 3. 22–end Phil. 3. 1–14	*EP*: Ps. 119. 41–56 Ecclus. 39. 1–10 *or* Isa. 56. 1–8 Col. 1.24 – 2.7

Day	Colour	Principal Service		Second Service	Third Service
26 Friday		**Timothy and Titus, Companions of Paul**			
	W	Isa. 61. 1–3a Ps. 100 2 Tim. 2. 1–8 *or* Titus 1. 1–5 Luke 10. 1–9	*or* 2 Sam. 11. 1–10, 13–17 Ps. 51. 1–6, 9 Mark 4. 26–34	Ps. 61; ***65*** *alt*. Ps. 139 Gen. ch. 16 Matt. 26. 57–end	Ps. ***67***; 77 *alt*. Ps. ***130***; 131; 137 Hos. 6.7 – 7.2 1 Cor. 11. 17–end
27 Saturday					
	W		2 Sam. 12. 1–7, 10–17 Ps. 51. 11–16 Mark 4. 35–end	Ps. 68 *alt*. Ps. 120; ***121***; 122 Gen. 17. 1–22 Matt. 27. 1–10	Ps. ***72***; 76 *alt*. Ps. 118 Hos. ch. 8 1 Cor. 12. 1–11 **ct**
28 Sunday		**THE FOURTH SUNDAY OF EPIPHANY** *or The Presentation of Christ in the Temple (Candlemas)**			
	W		Deut. 18. 15–20 Ps. 111 Rev. 12. 1–5a Mark 1. 21–28	Ps. 71. 1–6, 15–17 Jer. 1. 4–10 Mark 1. 40–end	Ps. 34 (*or* 34. 1–10) 1 Sam. 3. 1–20 1 Cor. 14. 12–20 *Gospel*: Matt. 13. 10–17

*See provision for First EP on 1 February and throughout the day for The Presentation on 2 February.

January/ February 2024			Sunday Principal Service Weekday Eucharist	Third Service Morning Prayer	Second Service Evening Prayer
29 Monday					
W [**G**]* **DEL 4**			2 Sam. 15. 13–14, 30; 16. 5–13 Ps. 3 Mark 5. 1–20	**Ps. ***57***; 96 *alt*. Ps. 123; 124; 125; ***126*** Gen. 18. 1–15 Matt. 27. 11–26	**Ps. 2; ***20*** *alt*. Ps. ***127***; 128; 129 Hos. ch. 9 1 Cor. 12. 12–end
30 Tuesday	**Charles, King and Martyr, 1649**				
Wr [**Gr**]	Com. Martyr *also* Ecclus. 2. 12–17 1 Tim. 6. 12–16	*or*	2 Sam. 18.9–10, 14, 24–25, 30 – 19.3 Ps. 86. 1–6 Mark. 5. 21–end	**Ps. ***93***; 97 *alt*. Ps. ***132***; 133 Gen. 18. 16–end Matt. 27. 27–44	**Ps. ***19***; 21 *alt*. Ps. (134); ***135*** Hos. ch. 10 1 Cor. ch. 13
31 Wednesday	*John Bosco, Priest, Founder of the Salesian Teaching Order, 1888*				
W [**G**]			2 Sam. 24. 2, 9–17 Ps. 32. 1–8 Mark 6. 1–6a	**Ps. ***95***; 98 *alt*. Ps. 119. 153–end Gen. 19. 1–3, 12–29 Matt. 27. 45–56	**Ps. ***81***; 111 *alt*. Ps. 136 Hos. 11. 1–11 1 Cor. 14. 1–19

1 Thursday *Brigid, Abbess of Kildare, c. 525*

W [G]	1 Kings 2. 1–4, 10–12 *Canticle*: 1 Chron. 29. 10–12 *or* Ps. 145. 1–5 Mark 6. 7–13	**Ps. 99; ***110*** *alt*. Ps. ***143***; 146 Gen. 21. 1–21 Matt. 27. 57–end	*First EP of The Presentation* Ps. 118 1 Sam. 1. 19b–end Heb. 4. 11–end **𝔚 ct** *or, if The Presentation was kept on 28 January*: Ps. ***138***; 140; 141 Hos. 11.12 – 12.end 1 Cor. 14. 20–end

*Ordinary Time begins today if The Presentation was observed on 28 January.
**If The Presentation was observed on 28 January, the alternative psalms are used.

February 2024		Sunday Principal Service Weekday Eucharist	Third Service Morning Prayer	Second Service Evening Prayer
2 Friday	**THE PRESENTATION OF CHRIST IN THE TEMPLE (CANDLEMAS)**			
𝔚		Mal. 3. 1–5 Ps. 24. [1–6] 7–end Heb. 2. 14–end Luke 2. 22–40	*MP*: Ps. ***48***; 146 Exod. 13. 1–16 Rom. 12. 1–5	*EP*: Ps. 122; ***132*** Hag. 2. 1–9 John 2. 18–22
	or, if The Presentation is observed on 28 January:			
G		Ecclus. 47. 2–11 Ps. 18. 31–36, 50–end Mark 6. 14–29	Ps. 142; ***144*** Gen. 22. 1–19 Matt. 28. 1–15	Ps. 145 Hos. 13. 1–14 1 Cor. 16. 1–9
3 Saturday	**Anskar, Archbishop of Hamburg, Missionary in Denmark and Sweden, 865** *Ordinary Time starts today (or on 29 January if The Presentation is observed on 28 January)*			
Gw	Com. Missionary *esp.* Isa. 52. 7–10 *also* Rom. 10. 11–15	*or* 1 Kings 3. 4–13 Ps. 119. 9–16 Mark 6. 30–34	Ps. 147 Gen. ch. 23 Matt. 28. 16–end	Ps. ***148***; 149; 150 Hos. ch. 14 1 Cor. 16. 10–end **ct**

4 Sunday	**THE SECOND SUNDAY BEFORE LENT**			
G		Prov. 8. 1, 22–31 Ps. 104. 26–end Col. 1. 15–20 John 1. 1–14	Ps. 29; 67 Deut. 8. 1–10 Matt. 6. 25–end	Ps. 65 Gen. 2. 4b–end Luke 8. 22–35
5 Monday				
G **DEL 5**		1 Kings 8. 1–7, 9–13 Ps. 132. 1–9 Mark 6. 53–end	Ps. ***1***; 2; 3 Gen. 29.31 – 30.24 2 Tim. 4. 1–8	Ps. ***4***; 7 Eccles. 7. 1–14 John 19. 1–16
6 Tuesday	*The Martyrs of Japan, 1597*			
G		1 Kings 8. 22–23, 27–30 Ps. 84. 1–10 Mark 7. 1–13	Ps. ***5***; 6; (8) Gen. 31. 1–24 2 Tim. 4. 9–end	Ps. ***9***; 10† Eccles. 7. 15–end John 19. 17–30
7 Wednesday				
G		1 Kings 10. 1–10 Ps. 37. 3–6, 30–32 Mark 7. 14–23	Ps. 119. 1–32 Gen. 31.25 – 32.2 Titus ch. 1	Ps. ***11***; 12; 13 Eccles. ch. 8 John 19. 31–end

February 2023		Sunday Principal Service Weekday Eucharist	Third Service Morning Prayer	Second Service Evening Prayer
8 Thursday				
G		1 Kings 11. 4–13 Ps. 106. 3, 35–41 Mark 7. 24–30	Ps. 14; ***15***; 16 Gen. 32. 3–30 Titus ch. 2	Ps. 18† Eccles. ch. 9 John 20. 1–10
9 Friday				
G		1 Kings 11. 29–32; 12. 19 Ps. 81. 8–14 Mark 7. 31–end	Ps. 17; ***19*** Gen. 33. 1–17 Titus ch. 3	Ps. 22 Eccles. 11. 1–8 John 20. 11–18
10 Saturday	*Scholastica, sister of Benedict, Abbess of Plombariola, c. 543*			
G		1 Kings 12.26–32; 13. 33–end Ps. 106. 6–7, 20–23 Mark 8. 1–10	Ps. 20; 21; ***23*** Gen. ch. 35 Philem.	Ps. ***24***; 25 Eccles. 11.9 – 12.end John 20. 19–end **ct**

11 Sunday **THE SUNDAY NEXT BEFORE LENT**			
G	2 Kings 2. 1–12 Ps. 50. 1–6 2 Cor. 4. 3–6 Mark 9. 2–9	Ps. 27; 150 Exod. 24. 12–end 2 Cor. 3. 12–end	Ps. 2; [99] 1 Kings 19. 1–16 2 Pet. 1. 16–end *Gospel*: Mark 9. [2–8] 9–13
12 Monday			
G **DEL 6**	Jas. 1. 1–11 Ps. 119. 65–72 Mark 8. 11–13	Ps. 27; ***30*** Gen. 37. 1–11 Gal. ch. 1	Ps. 26; ***28***; 29 Jer. ch. 1 John 3. 1–21
13 Tuesday			
G	Jas. 1. 12–18 Ps. 94. 12–18 Mark 8. 14–21	Ps. 32; ***36*** Gen. 37. 12–end Gal. 2. 1–10	Ps. 33 Jer. 2. 1–13 John 3. 22–end
14 Wednesday **ASH WEDNESDAY**			
P	Joel 2. 1–2, 12–17 *or* Isa. 58. 1–12 Ps. 51. 1–18 2 Cor. 5.20b – 6.10 Matt. 6. 1–6, 16–21 *or* John 8. 1–11	*MP*: Ps. 38 Dan. 9. 3–6, 17–19 1 Tim. 6. 6–19	*EP*: Ps. ***51*** *or* Ps. 102 (*or* 102. 1–18) Isa. 1. 10–18 Luke 15. 11–end

February 2024		Sunday Principal Service Weekday Eucharist	Third Service Morning Prayer	Second Service Evening Prayer
15 Thursday	*Sigfrid, Bishop, Apostle of Sweden, 1045; Thomas Bray, Priest, Founder of the SPCK and the SPG, 1730*			
P		Deut. 30. 15–end Ps. 1 Luke 9. 22–25	Ps. 77 *alt.* Ps. 37† Gen. ch. 39 Gal. 2. 11–end	Ps. 74 *alt.* Ps. 39; ***40*** Jer. 2. 14–32 John 4. 1–26
16 Friday				
P		Isa. 58. 1–9a Ps. 51. 1–5, 17–18 Matt. 9. 14–15	Ps. **3**; 7 *alt.* Ps. 31 Gen. ch. 40 Gal. 3. 1–14	Ps. 31 *alt.* Ps. 35 Jer. 3. 6–22 John 4. 27–42
17 Saturday	**Janani Luwum, Archbishop of Uganda, Martyr, 1977**			
Pr	Com. Martyr *also* Ecclus. 4. 20–28 John 12. 24–32 *or*	Isa. 58. 9b–end Ps. 86. 1–7 Luke 5. 27–32	Ps. 71 *alt.* Ps. 41; ***42***; 43 Gen. 41. 1–24 Gal. 3. 15–22	Ps. 73 *alt.* Ps. 45; ***46*** Jer. 4. 1–18 John 4. 43–end **ct**

18 Sunday **THE FIRST SUNDAY OF LENT**			
P	Gen. 9. 8–17 Ps. 25. 1–9 1 Pet. 3. 18–end Mark 1. 9–15	Ps. 77 Exod. 34. 1–10 Rom. 10. 8b–13	Ps. 119. 17–32 Gen. 2. 15–17; 3. 1–7 Rom. 5. 12–19 *or* Luke 13. 31–end
19 Monday			
P	Lev. 19. 1–2, 11–18 Ps. 19. 7–end Matt. 25. 31–end	Ps. 10; ***11*** *alt.* Ps. 44 Gen. 41. 25–45 Gal. 3.23 – 4.7	Ps. 12; ***13***; 14 *alt.* Ps. ***47***; 49 Jer. 4. 19–end John 5. 1–18
20 Tuesday			
P	Isa. 55. 10–11 Ps. 34. 4–6, 21–22 Matt. 6. 7–15	Ps. 44 *alt.* Ps. ***48***; 52 Gen. 41.46 – 42.5 Gal. 4. 8–20	Ps. 46; ***49*** *alt.* Ps. 50 Jer. 5. 1–19 John 5. 19–29
21 Wednesday Ember Day			
P	Jonah ch. 3 Ps. 51. 1–5, 17–18 Luke 11. 29–32	Ps. ***6***; 17 *alt.* Ps. 119. 57–80 Gen. 42. 6–17 Gal. 4.21 – 5.1	Ps. 9; ***28*** *alt.* Ps. ***59***; 60 (67) Jer. 5. 20–end John 5. 30–end

February 2024		Sunday Principal Service Weekday Eucharist	Third Service Morning Prayer	Second Service Evening Prayer
22 Thursday				
P		Esth. 14. 1–5, 12–14 *or* Isa. 55. 6–9 Ps. 138 Matt. 7. 7–12	Ps. ***42***; 43 *alt*. Ps. 56; ***57***; (63†) Gen. 42. 18–28 Gal. 5. 2–15	Ps. 137; 138; ***142*** *alt*. Ps. 61; ***62***; 64 Jer. 6. 9–21 John 6. 1–15
23 Friday	**Polycarp, Bishop of Smyrna, Martyr, *c.* 155** Ember Day			
Pr	Com. Martyr *also* Rev. 2. 8–11 *or*	Ezek. 18. 21–28 Ps. 130 Matt. 5. 20–26	Ps. 22 *alt*. Ps. ***51***; 54 Gen. 42. 29–end Gal. 5. 16–end	Ps. 54; ***55*** *alt*. Ps. 38 Jer. 6. 22–end John 6. 16–27
24 Saturday*	Ember Day			
P		Deut. 26. 16–end Ps. 119. 1–8 Matt. 5. 43–end	Ps. 59; ***63*** *alt*. Ps. 68 Gen. 43. 1–15 Gal. ch. 6	Ps. ***4***; 16 *alt*. Ps. 65; ***66*** Jer. 7. 1–20 John 6. 27–40 **ct**

25 Sunday	**THE SECOND SUNDAY OF LENT**				
P			Gen. 17. 1–7, 15–16 Ps. 22. 23–end Rom. 4. 13–end Mark 8. 31–end	Ps. 105. 1–6, 37–end Isa. 51. 1–11 Gal. 3. 1–9, 23–end	Ps. 135 (*or* 135. 1–14) Gen. 12. 1–9 Heb. 11. 1–3, 8–16 *Gospel*: John 8. 51–end
26 Monday					
P			Dan. 9. 4–10 Ps. 79. 8–9, 12, 14 Luke 6. 36–38	Ps. 26; ***32*** *alt.* Ps. 71 Gen. 43. 16–end Heb. ch. 1	Ps. 70; ***74*** *alt.* Ps. ***72***; 75 Jer. 7. 21–end John 6. 41–51
27 Tuesday	**George Herbert, Priest, Poet, 1633**				
Pw	Com. Pastor *esp.* Mal. 2. 5–7 Matt. 11. 25–30 *also* Rev. 19. 5–9	*or*	Isa. 1. 10, 16–20 Ps. 50. 8, 16–end Matt. 23. 1–12	Ps. 50 *alt.* Ps. 73 Gen. 44. 1–17 Heb. 2. 1–9	Ps. ***52***; 53; 54 *alt.* Ps. 74 Jer. 8. 1–15 John 6. 52–59

*Matthias may be celebrated on 24 February instead of 14 May.

		Sunday Principal Service Weekday Eucharist	Third Service Morning Prayer	Second Service Evening Prayer
28 Wednesday				
P		Jer. 18. 18–20 Ps. 31. 4–5, 14–18 Matt. 20. 17–28	Ps. 35 *alt.* Ps. 77 Gen. 44. 18–end Heb. 2. 10–end	Ps. ***3***; 51 *alt.* Ps. 119. 81–104 Jer. 8.18 – 9.11 John 6. 60–end
29 Thursday				
P		Jer. 17. 5–10 Ps. 1 Luke 16. 19–end	Ps. 34 *alt.* Ps. 78. 1–39† Gen. 45. 1–15 Heb. 3. 1–6	Ps. 71 *alt.* Ps. 78. 40–end† Jer. 9. 12–24 John 7. 1–13

March 2024

1 Friday	**David, Bishop of Menevia, Patron of Wales, c. 601**			
Pw	Com. Bishop *also* 2 Sam. 23. 1–4 Ps. 89. 19–22, 24	*or* Gen. 37. 3–4, 12–13, 17–28 Ps. 105. 16–22 Matt. 21. 33–43, 45–46	Ps. 40; ***41*** *alt.* Ps. 55 Gen. 45. 16–end Heb. 3. 7–end	Ps. ***6***; 38 *alt.* Ps. 69 Jer. 10. 1–16 John 7. 14–24

2 Saturday	**Chad, Bishop of Lichfield, Missionary, 672***				
Pw	Com. Missionary *also* 1 Tim. 6. 11b–16	*or*	Mic. 7. 14–15, 18–20 Ps. 103. 1–4, 9–12 Luke 15. 1–3, 11–end	Ps. 3; ***25*** *alt.* Ps. ***76***; 79 Gen. 46. 1–7, 28–end Heb. 4. 1–13	Ps. ***23***; 27 *alt.* Ps. 81; ***84*** Jer. 10. 17–24 John 7. 25–36 **ct**
3 Sunday	**THE THIRD SUNDAY OF LENT**				
P			Exod. 20. 1–17 Ps. 19 (*or* 19. 7–end) 1 Cor. 1. 18–25 John 2. 13–22	Ps. 18. 1–25 Jer. ch. 38 Phil. 1. 1–26	Ps. 11; 12 Exod. 5.1 – 6.1 Phil. 3. 4b–14 *or* Matt. 10. 16–22
4 Monday**					
P			2 Kings 5. 1–15 Ps. 42. 1–2; 43. 1–4 Luke 4. 24–30	Ps. ***5***; 7 *alt.* Ps. ***80***; 82 Gen. 47. 1–27 Heb. 4.14 – 5.10	Ps. 11; ***17*** *alt.* Ps. ***85***; 86 Jer. 11. 1–17 John 7. 37–52

*Chad may be celebrated with Cedd on 26 October instead of 2 March.
**The following readings may replace those provided for Holy Communion on any day during the Third Week of Lent: Exod. 17. 1–7; Ps. 95. 1–2, 6–end; John 4. 5–42.

March 2023		Sunday Principal Service Weekday Eucharist	Third Service Morning Prayer	Second Service Evening Prayer
5 Tuesday				
P		Song of the Three 2, 11–20 *or* Dan. 2. 20–23 Ps. 25. 3–10 Matt. 18. 21–end	Ps. 6; ***9*** *alt.* Ps. 87; ***89. 1–18*** Gen. 47.28 – 48.end Heb. 5.11 – 6.12	Ps. 61; 62; ***64*** *alt.* Ps. 89. 19–end Jer. 11.18 – 12.6 John 7.53 – 8.11
6 Wednesday				
P		Deut. 4. 1, 5–9 Ps. 147. 13–end Matt. 5. 17–19	Ps. 38 *alt.* Ps. 119. 105–128 Gen. 49. 1–32 Heb. 6. 13–end	Ps. 36; ***39*** *alt.* Ps. ***91***; 93 Jer. 13. 1–11 John 8. 12–30
7 Thursday	**Perpetua, Felicity and their Companions, Martyrs at Carthage, 203**			
Pr	Com. Martyr *esp.* Rev. 12. 10–12a *also* Wisd. 3. 1–7	*or* Jer. 7. 23–28 Ps. 95. 1–2, 6–end Luke 11. 14–23	Ps. ***56***; 57 *alt.* Ps. 90; ***92*** Gen. 49.33 – 50.end Heb. 7. 1–10	Ps. ***59***; 60 *alt.* Ps. 94 Jer. ch. 14 John 8. 31–47

8 Friday	**Edward King, Bishop of Lincoln, 1910** *Felix, Bishop, Apostle to the East Angles, 647; Geoffrey Studdert Kennedy, Priest, Poet, 1929*			
Pw	Com. Bishop *also* Heb. 13. 1–8	*or* Hos. ch. 14 Ps. 81. 6–10, 13, 16 Mark 12. 28–34	Ps. 22 *alt.* Ps. ***88***; (95) Exod. 1. 1–14 Heb. 7. 11–end	Ps. 69 *alt.* Ps. 102 Jer. 15. 10–end John 8. 48–end
9 Saturday				
P		Hos. 5.15 – 6.6 Ps. 51. 1–2, 17–end Luke 18. 9–14	Ps. 31 *alt.* Ps. 96; ***97***; 100 Exod. 1.22 – 2.10 Heb. ch. 8	Ps. ***116***; 130 *alt.* Ps. 104 Jer. 16.10 – 17.4 John 9. 1–17 **ct**

March 2024		Sunday Principal Service Weekday Eucharist	Third Service Morning Prayer	Second Service Evening Prayer
10 Sunday	**THE FOURTH SUNDAY OF LENT** (Mothering Sunday)			
P		Num. 21. 4–9 Ps. 107. 1–3, 17–22 (*or* 107. 1–9) Eph. 2. 1–10 John 3. 14–21	Ps. 27 1 Sam. 16. 1–13 John 9. 1–25	Ps. 13; 14 Exod. 6. 2–13 Rom. 5. 1–11 *Gospel*: John 12. 1–8 If the Principal Service readings for The Fourth Sunday of Lent are displaced by Mothering Sunday provisions, they may be used at the Second Service.
	or, for Mothering Sunday			
		Exod. 2. 1–10 *or* 1 Sam. 1. 20–end Ps. 34. 11–20 *or* Ps. 127. 1–4 2 Cor. 1. 3–7 *or* Col. 3. 12–17 Luke 2. 33–35 *or* John 19. 25b–27		

11 Monday*			
P	Isa. 65. 17–21 Ps. 30. 1–5, 8, 11–end John 4. 43–end	Ps. 70; ***77*** *alt.* Ps. **98**; 99; 101 Exod. 2. 11–22 Heb. 9. 1–14	Ps. ***25***; 28 *alt.* Ps. ***105***† (*or* 103) Jer. 17. 5–18 John 9. 18–end
12 Tuesday			
P	Ezek. 47. 1–9, 12 Ps. 46. 1–8 John 5. 1–3, 5–16	Ps. 54; ***79*** *alt.* Ps. ***106***† (*or* 103) Exod. 2.23 – 3.20 Heb. 9. 15–end	Ps. ***80***; 82 *alt.* Ps. 107† Jer. 18. 1–12 John 10. 1–10
13 Wednesday			
P	Isa. 49. 8–15 Ps. 145. 8–18 John 5. 17–30	Ps. **63**; *90* *alt.* Ps. 110; ***111***; 112 Exod. 4. 1–23 Heb. 10. 1–18	Ps. 52; ***91*** *alt.* Ps. 119. 129–152 Jer. 18. 13–end John 10. 11–21

*The following readings may replace those provided for Holy Communion on any day during the Fourth Week of Lent: Mic. 7. 7–9; Ps. 27. 1, 9–10, 16–17; John ch. 9.

March 2024		Sunday Principal Service Weekday Eucharist	Third Service Morning Prayer	Second Service Evening Prayer
14 Thursday				
P		Exod. 32. 7–14 Ps. 106. 19–23 John 5. 31–end	Ps. 53; ***86*** *alt*. Ps. 113; ***115*** Exod. 4.27 – 6.1 Heb. 10. 19–25	Ps. 94 *alt*. Ps. 114; ***116***; 117 Jer. 19. 1–13 John 10. 22–end
15 Friday				
P		Wisd. 2. 1, 12–22 *or* Jer. 26. 8–11 Ps. 34. 15–end John 7. 1–2, 10, 25–30	Ps. 102 *alt*. Ps. 139 Exod. 6. 2–13 Heb. 10. 26–end	Ps. 13; ***16*** *alt*. Ps. ***130***; 131; 137 Jer. 19.14 – 20.6 John 11. 1–16
16 Saturday				
P		Jer. 11. 18–20 Ps. 7. 1–2, 8–10 John 7. 40–52	Ps. 32 *alt*. Ps. 120; ***121***; 122 Exod. 7. 8–end Heb. 11. 1–16	Ps. ***140***; 141; 142 *alt*. Ps. 118 Jer. 20. 7–end John 11. 17–27 **ct**

17 Sunday **THE FIFTH SUNDAY OF LENT (Passiontide begins)**

P	Jer. 31. 31–34 Ps. 51. 1–13 *or* Ps. 119. 9–16 Heb. 5. 5–10 John 12. 20–33	Ps. 107. 1–22 Exod. 24. 3–8 Heb. 12. 18–end	Ps. 34 (*or* 34. 1–10) Exod. 7. 8–24 Rom. 5. 12–end *Gospel*: Luke 22. 1–13

18 Monday* *Cyril, Bishop of Jerusalem, Teacher, 386*

P	Susanna 1–9, 15–17, 19–30, 33–62 (*or* 41b–62) *or* Josh. 2. 1–14 Ps. 23 John 8. 1–11	Ps. ***73***; 121 *alt*. Ps. 123; 124; 125; ***126*** Exod. 8. 1–19 Heb. 11. 17–31	Ps. ***26***; 27 *alt*. Ps. ***127***; 128; 129 Jer. 21. 1–10 John 11. 28–44 *or First EP of Joseph* Ps. 132 Hos. 11. 1–9 Luke 2. 41–end **W ct**

*The following readings may replace those provided for Holy Communion on any day, except St Joseph's Day, during the Fifth Week of Lent: 2 Kings 4. 18–21, 32–37; Ps. 17. 1–8, 16; John 11. 1–45.

March 2024			Sunday Principal Service Weekday Eucharist	Third Service Morning Prayer	Second Service Evening Prayer
19 Tuesday	**JOSEPH OF NAZARETH**				
W			2 Sam. 7. 4–16 Ps. 89. 26–36 Rom. 4. 13–18 Matt. 1. 18–end	*MP*: Ps. 25; 147. 1–12 Isa. 11. 1–10 Matt. 13. 54–end	*EP*: Ps. 1; 112 Gen. 50. 22–end Matt. 2. 13–end
20 Wednesday	**Cuthbert, Bishop of Lindisfarne, Missionary, 687***				
Pw	Com. Missionary *esp.* Ezek. 34. 11–16 *also* Matt. 18. 12–14	*or*	Dan. 3. 14–20, 24–25, 28 *Canticle*: Bless the Lord John 8. 31–42	Ps. ***55***; 124 *alt.* Ps. 119. 153–end Exod. 9. 1–12 Heb. 12. 3–13	Ps. 56; ***62*** *alt.* Ps. 136 Jer. 22.20 – 23.8 John 12. 1–11
21 Thursday	**Thomas Cranmer, Archbishop of Canterbury, Reformation Martyr, 1556**				
Pr	Com. Martyr	*or*	Gen. 17. 3–9 Ps. 105. 4–9 John 8. 51–end	Ps. ***40***; 125 *alt.* Ps. ***143***; 146 Exod. 9. 13–end Heb. 12. 14–end	Ps. 42; ***43*** *alt.* Ps. ***138***; 140; 141 Jer. 23. 9–32 John 12. 12–19

22 Friday				
P		Jer. 20. 10–13 Ps. 18. 1–6 John 10. 31–end	Ps. ***22***; 126 *alt.* Ps. 142; ***144*** Exod. ch. 10 Heb. 13. 1–16	Ps. 31 *alt.* Ps. 145 Jer. ch. 24 John 12. 20–36a
23 Saturday				
P		Ezek. 37. 21–end *Canticle*: Jer. 31. 10–13 *or* Ps. 121 John 11. 45–end	Ps. ***23***; 127 *alt.* Ps. 147 Exod. ch. 11 Heb. 13. 17–end	Ps. 128; 129; ***130*** *alt.* Ps. ***148***; 149; 150 Jer. 25. 1–14 John 12. 36b–end **ct**
24 Sunday	**PALM SUNDAY**			
R	*Liturgy of the Palms* Mark 11. 1–11 *or* John 12. 12–16 Ps. 118. 1–2, 19–end (*or* 118. 19–end)	*Liturgy of the Passion* Isa. 50. 4–9a Ps. 31. 9–16 (*or* 31. 9–18) Phil. 2. 5–11 Mark 14.1 - 15.end *or* Mark 15. 1–39 [40–end]	Ps. 61; 62 Zech. 9. 9–12 1 Cor. 2. 1–12	Ps. 69. 1–20 Isa. 5. 1–7 Mark 12. 1–12

*Cuthbert may be celebrated on 4 September instead of 20 March.

March 2024		Sunday Principal Service Weekday Eucharist	Third Service Morning Prayer	Second Service Evening Prayer
25 Monday	**MONDAY OF HOLY WEEK** (The Annunciation transferred to 8 April)			
R		Isa. 42. 1–9 Ps. 36. 5–11 Heb. 9. 11–15 John 12. 1–11	*MP*: Ps. 41 Lam. 1. 1–12a Luke 22. 1–23	*EP*: Ps. 25 Lam. 2. 8–19 Col. 1. 18–23
26 Tuesday	**TUESDAY OF HOLY WEEK**			
R		Isa. 49. 1–7 Ps. 71. 1–14 (*or* 71. 1–8) 1 Cor. 1. 18–31 John 12. 20–36	*MP*: Ps. 27 Lam. 3. 1–18 Luke 22. [24–38] 39–53	*EP*: Ps. 55. 13–24 Lam. 3. 40–51 Gal. 6. 11–end
27 Wednesday	**WEDNESDAY OF HOLY WEEK**			
R		Isa. 50. 4–9a Ps. 70 Heb. 12. 1–3 John 13. 21–32	*MP*: Ps. 102 (*or* 102. 1–18) Wisd. 1.16 – 2.1, 12–22 *or* Jer. 11. 18–20 Luke 22. 54–end	*EP*: Ps. 88 Isa. 63. 1–9 Rev. 14.18 – 15.4

28 Thursday	**MAUNDY THURSDAY**			
W(HC)R		Exod. 12. 1–4 [5–10], 11–14 Ps. 116. 1, 10–end (*or* 116. 9–end) 1 Cor. 11. 23–26 John 13. 1–17, 31b–35	*MP*: Ps. 42; 43 Lev. 16. 2–24 Luke 23. 1–25	*EP*: Ps. 39 Exod. ch. 11 Eph. 2. 11–18
29 Friday	**GOOD FRIDAY**			
R		Isa. 52.13 – 53.end Ps. 22 (*or* 22. 1–11 *or* 22. 1–21) Heb. 10. 16–25 *or* Heb. 4. 14–16; 5. 7–9 John 18.1 – 19.end	*MP*: Ps. 69 Gen. 22. 1–18 *A part of* John 18 – 19 *if not read at the Principal Service* *or* Heb. 10. 1–10	*EP*: Ps. 130; 143 Lam. 5. 15–end *A part of* John 18 – 19 *if not read at the Principal Service, especially* John 19. 38–end *or* Col. 1. 18–23
30 Saturday	**EASTER EVE**			
	These readings are for use at services other than the Easter Vigil	Job 14. 1–14 *or* Lam. 3. 1–9, 19–24 Ps. 31. 1–4, 15–16 (*or* 31. 1–5) 1 Pet. 4. 1–8 Matt. 27. 57–end *or* John 19. 38–end	Ps. 142 Hos. 6. 1–6 John 2. 18–22	Ps. 116 Job 19. 21–27 1 John 5. 5–12

March/April 2024		Sunday Principal Service Weekday Eucharist	Third Service Morning Prayer	Second Service Evening Prayer
31 Sunday	**EASTER DAY**			
𝔚	*The following readings and psalms (or canticles) are provided for use at the Easter Vigil. A minimum of three Old Testament readings should be chosen. The reading from Exodus ch. 14 should always be used.*	Gen. 1.1 – 2.4a & Ps. 136. 1–9, 23–end Gen. 7. 1–5, 11–18; 8. 6–18; 9. 8–13 & Ps. 46 Gen. 22. 1–18 & Ps. 16 Exod. 14. 10–end; 15. 20–21 & *Canticle*: Exod. 15. 1b–13, 17–18 Isa. 55. 1–11 & *Canticle*: Isa. 12. 2–end Baruch 3.9–15, 32 – 4.4 & Ps. 19 *or* Prov. 8. 1–8, 19–21; 9. 4b–6 & Ps. 19 Ezek. 36. 24–28 & Ps. 42; 43 Ezek. 37. 1–14 & Ps. 143 Zeph. 3. 14–end & Ps. 98 Rom. 6. 3–11 & Ps. 114 Mark 16. 1–8		
𝔚	*Easter Day Services* *The reading from Acts must be used as either the first or second reading at the Principal Service.*	Acts 10. 34–43 *or* Isa. 25. 6–9 Ps. 118. 1–2, 14–24 (*or* 118. 14–24) 1 Cor. 15. 1–11 *or* Acts 10. 34–43 John 20. 1–18 *or* Mark 16. 1–8	*MP*: Ps. 114; 117 Gen. 1. 1–5, 26–end 2 Cor. 5.14 – 6.2	*EP*: Ps. 105 *or* Ps. 66. 1–11 Ezek. 37. 1–14 Luke 24. 13–35

April 2024

1 Monday **MONDAY OF EASTER WEEK**

W	Acts 2. 14, 22–32 Ps. 16. 1–2, 6–end Matt. 28. 8–15	Ps. ***111***; 117; 146 Exod. 12. 1–14 1 Cor. 15. 1–11	Ps. 135 Song of Sol. 1.9 – 2.7 Mark 16. 1–8

2 Tuesday **TUESDAY OF EASTER WEEK**

W	Acts 2. 36–41 Ps. 33. 4–5, 18–end John 20. 11–18	Ps. ***112***; 147. 1–12 Exod. 12. 14–36 1 Cor. 15. 12–19	Ps. 136 Song of Sol. 2. 8–end Luke 24. 1–12

3 Wednesday **WEDNESDAY OF EASTER WEEK**

W	Acts 3. 1–10 Ps. 105. 1–9 Luke 24. 13–35	Ps. ***113***; 147. 13–end Exod. 12. 37–end 1 Cor. 15. 20–28	Ps. 105 Song of Sol. ch. 3 Matt. 28. 16–end

4 Thursday **THURSDAY OF EASTER WEEK**

W	Acts 3. 11–end Ps. 8 Luke 24. 35–48	Ps. ***114***; 148 Exod. 13. 1–16 1 Cor. 15. 29–34	Ps. 106 Song of Sol. 5.2 – 6.3 Luke 7. 11–17

April 2023		Sunday Principal Service Weekday Eucharist	Third Service Morning Prayer	Second Service Evening Prayer
5 Friday	**FRIDAY OF EASTER WEEK**			
W		Acts 4. 1–12 Ps. 118. 1–4, 22–26 John 21. 1–14	Ps. ***115***; 149 Exod. 13.17 – 14.14 1 Cor. 15. 35–50	Ps. 107 Song of Sol. 7.10 – 8.4 Luke 8. 41–end
6 Saturday	**SATURDAY OF EASTER WEEK**			
W		Acts 4. 13–21 Ps. 118. 1–4, 14–21 Mark 16. 9–15	Ps. ***116***; 150 Exod. 14. 15–end 1 Cor. 15. 51–end	Ps. 145 Song of Sol. 8. 5–7 John 11. 17–44 **ct**
7 Sunday	**THE SECOND SUNDAY OF EASTER**			
W	*The reading from Acts must be used as either the first or second reading at the Principal Service.*	Acts 4. 32–35 [*or* Exod. 14. 10–end; 15. 20–21] Ps. 133 1 John 1.1 – 2.2 John 20. 19–end	Ps. 22. 20–end Isa. 53. 6–12 Rom. 4. 13–25	*First EP of The Annunciation* Ps. 85 Wisd. 9. 1–12 *or* Gen. 3. 8–15 Gal. 4. 1–5 **𝔚 ct**

8 Monday	**THE ANNUNCIATION OF OUR LORD TO THE BLESSED VIRGIN MARY** (transferred from 25 March)				
𝔚			Isa. 7. 10–14 Ps. 40. 5–11 Heb. 10. 4–10 Luke 1. 26–38	*MP*: Ps. 111; 113 1 Sam. 2. 1–10 Rom. 5. 12–end	*EP*: Ps. 131; 146 Isa. 52. 1–12 Heb. 2. 5–end
9 Tuesday	*Dietrich Bonhoeffer, Lutheran Pastor, Martyr, 1945*				
W			Acts 4. 32–end Ps. 93 John 3. 7–15	Ps. ***8***; 20; 21 *alt*. Ps. ***5***; 6; (8) Exod. 15.22 – 16.10 Col. 1. 15–end	Ps. 104 *alt*. Ps. 9; ***10***† Deut. 1. 19–40 John 20. 11–18
10 Wednesday	**William Law, Priest, Spiritual Writer, 1761** *William of Ockham, Friar, Philosopher, Teacher, 1347*				
W	Com. Teacher *esp*. 1 Cor. 2. 9–end *also* Matt. 17. 1–9	*or*	Acts 5. 17–26 Ps. 34. 1–8 John 3. 16–21	Ps. 16; ***30*** *alt*. Ps. 119. 1–32 Exod. 16. 11–end Col. 2. 1–15	Ps. 33 *alt*. Ps. ***11***; 12; 13 Deut. 3. 18–end John 20. 19–end

		Sunday Principal Service Weekday Eucharist	Third Service Morning Prayer	Second Service Evening Prayer
11 Thursday	*George Augustus Selwyn, first Bishop of New Zealand, 1878*			
W		Acts 5. 27–33 Ps. 34. 1, 15–end John 3. 31–end	Ps. ***28***; 29 *alt*. Ps. 14; ***15***; 16 Exod. ch. 17 Col. 2.16 – 3.11	Ps. 34 *alt*. Ps. 18† Deut. 4. 1–14 John 21. 1–14
12 Friday				
W		Acts 5. 34–42 Ps. 27. 1–5, 16–17 John 6. 1–15	Ps. 57; ***61*** *alt*. Ps. 17; ***19*** Exod. 18. 1–12 Col. 3.12 – 4.1	Ps. 118 *alt*. Ps. 22 Deut. 4. 15–31 John 21. 15–19
13 Saturday				
W		Acts 6. 1–7 Ps. 33. 1–5, 18–19 John 6. 16–21	Ps. 63; ***84*** *alt*. Ps. 20; 21; ***23*** Exod. 18. 13–end Col. 4. 2–end	Ps. 66 *alt*. Ps. ***24***; 25 Deut. 4. 32–40 John 21. 20–end **ct**

14 Sunday	**THE THIRD SUNDAY OF EASTER**			
W	*The reading from Acts must be used as either the first or second reading at the Principal Service.*	Acts 3. 12–19 [or Zeph. 3. 14–end] Ps. 4 1 John 3. 1–7 Luke 24. 36b–48	Ps. 77. 11–20 Isa. 63. 7–15 1 Cor. 10. 1–13	Ps. 142 Deut. 7. 7–13 Rev. 2. 1–11 *Gospel*: Luke 16. 19–end
15 Monday				
W		Acts 6. 8–15 Ps. 119. 17–24 John 6. 22–29	Ps. ***96***; 97 *alt.* Ps. 27; ***30*** Exod. ch. 19 Luke 1. 1–25	Ps. ***61***; 65 *alt.* Ps. 26; ***28***; 29 Deut. 5. 1–22 Eph. 1. 1–14
16 Tuesday	*Isabella Gilmore, Deaconess, 1923*			
W		Acts 7.51 – 8.1a Ps. 31. 1–5, 16 John 6. 30–35	Ps. ***98***; 99; 100 *alt.* Ps. 32; ***36*** Exod. 20. 1–21 Luke 1. 26–38	Ps. 71 *alt.* Ps. 33 Deut. 5. 22–end Eph. 1. 15–end

		Sunday Principal Service Weekday Eucharist	Third Service Morning Prayer	Second Service Evening Prayer
17 Wednesday				
W		Acts 8. 1b–8 Ps. 66. 1–6 John 6. 35–40	Ps. 105 *alt*. Ps. 34 Exod. ch. 24 Luke 1. 39–56	Ps. 67; ***72*** *alt*. Ps. 119. 33–56 Deut. ch. 6 Eph. 2. 1–10
18 Thursday				
W		Acts 8. 26–end Ps. 66. 7–8, 14–end John 6. 44–51	Ps. 136 *alt*. Ps. 37† Exod. 25. 1–22 Luke 1. 57–end	Ps. 73 *alt*. Ps. 39; ***40*** Deut. 7. 1–11 Eph. 2. 11–end
19 Friday	**Alphege, Archbishop of Canterbury, Martyr, 1012**			
Wr	Com. Martyr *also* Heb. 5. 1–4 *or*	Acts 9. 1–20 Ps. 117 John 6. 52–59	Ps. 107 *alt*. Ps. 31 Exod. 28. 1–4a, 29–38 Luke 2. 1–20	Ps. 77 *alt*. Ps. 35 Deut. 7. 12–end Eph. 3. 1–13

20 Saturday				
W		Acts 9. 31–42 Ps. 116. 10–15 John 6. 60–69	Ps. 108; ***110***; 111 *alt.* Ps. 41; ***42***; 43 Exod. 29. 1-9 Luke 2. 21–40	Ps. 23; ***27*** *alt.* Ps. 45; ***46*** Deut. ch. 8 Eph. 3. 14–end **ct**
21 Sunday	THE FOURTH SUNDAY OF EASTER			
W	*The reading from Acts must be used as either the first or second reading at the Principal Service.*	Acts 4. 5–12 [Gen. 7. 1–5, 11–18; 8. 6–18; 9. 8–13] Ps. 23 1 John 3. 16–end John 10. 11–18	Ps. 119. 89–96 Neh. 7.73b – 8.12 Luke 24. 25–32	Ps. 81. 8–16 Exod. 16. 4–15 Rev. 2. 12–17 *Gospel*: John 6. 30–40

April 2024		Sunday Principal Service Weekday Eucharist	Third Service Morning Prayer	Second Service Evening Prayer
22 Monday				
W		Acts 11. 1–18 Ps. 42. 1–2; 43. 1–4 John 10. 1–10 (*or* 11–18)	Ps. 103 *alt.* Ps. 44 Exod. 32. 1–14 Luke 2. 41–end	Ps. 112; 113; ***114*** *alt.* Ps. ***47***; 49 Deut. 9. 1–21 Eph. 4. 1–16 *or First EP of George* Ps. 111; 116 Jer. 15. 15–end Heb. 11.32 – 12.2 **R ct**
23 Tuesday	**GEORGE, MARTYR, PATRON OF ENGLAND, *c.* 304**			
R		1 Macc. 2. 59–64 *or* Rev. 12. 7–12 Ps. 126 2 Tim. 2. 3–13 John 15. 18–21	*MP*: Ps. 5; 146 Josh. 1. 1–9 Eph. 6. 10–20	*EP*: Ps. 3; 11 Isa. 43. 1–7 John 15. 1–8

24 Wednesday *Mellitus, Bishop of London, first Bishop at St Paul's, 624; The Seven Martyrs of the Melanesian Brotherhood, Solomon Islands, 2003*

W	Acts 12.24 – 13.5 Ps. 67 John 12. 44–end	Ps. 135 *alt*. Ps. 119. 57–80 Exod. ch. 33 Luke 3. 15–22	Ps. ***47***; 48 *alt*. Ps. ***59***; 60 (67) Deut. 10. 12–end Eph. 5. 1–14 *or First EP of Mark* Ps. 19 Isa. 52. 7–10 Mark 1. 1–15 **R ct**

25 Thursday **MARK THE EVANGELIST**

R	Prov. 15. 28–end *or* Acts 15. 35–end Ps. 119. 9–16 Eph. 4. 7–16 Mark 13. 5–13	*MP*: Ps. 37. 23–end; 148 Isa. 62. 6–10 *or* Ecclus. 51. 13–end Acts 12.25 – 13.13	*EP*: Ps. 45 Ezek. 1. 4–14 2 Tim. 4. 1–11

26 Friday

W	Acts 13. 26–33 Ps. 2 John 14. 1–6	Ps. 33 *alt*. Ps. ***51***; 54 Exod. 35.20 – 36.7 Luke 4. 14–30	Ps. ***36***; 40 *alt*. Ps. 38 Deut. 12. 1–14 Eph. 6. 1–9

April/May 2024		Sunday Principal Service Weekday Eucharist	Third Service Morning Prayer	Second Service Evening Prayer
27 Saturday	*Christina Rossetti, Poet, 1894*			
W		Acts 13. 44–end Ps. 98. 1–5 John 14. 7–14	Ps. 34 *alt*. Ps. 68 Exod. 40. 17–end Luke 4. 31–37	Ps. ***84***; 86 *alt*. Ps. 65; ***66*** Deut. 15. 1–18 Eph. 6. 10–end **ct**
28 Sunday	**THE FIFTH SUNDAY OF EASTER**			
W	*The reading from Acts must be used as either the first or second reading at the Principal Service.*	Acts 8. 26–end [Baruch 3.9–15, 32 – 4.4 *or* Gen. 22. 1–18] Ps. 22. 25–end 1 John 4. 7–end John 15. 1–8	Ps. 44. 16–end 2 Macc. 7. 7–14 *or* Dan. 3. 16–28 Heb. 11.32 – 12.2	Ps. 96 Isa. 60. 1–14 Rev. 3. 1–13 *Gospel*: Mark 16. 9–16
29 Monday	**Catherine of Siena, Teacher, 1380**			
W	Com. Teacher *or* *also* Prov. 8. 1, 6–11 John 17. 12–end	Acts 14. 5–18 Ps. 118. 1–3, 14–15 John 14. 21–26	Ps. 145 *alt*. Ps. 71 Num. 9. 15–end; 10. 33–end Luke 4. 38–end	Ps. 105 *alt*. Ps. ***72***; 75 Deut. 16. 1–20 1 Pet. 1. 1–12

30 Tuesday *Pandita Mary Ramabai, Translator of the Scriptures, 1922*

W	Acts 14. 19–end Ps. 145. 10–end John 14. 27–end	Ps. ***19***; 147. 1–12 *alt*. Ps. 73 Num. 11. 1–33 Luke 5. 1–11	Ps. 96; **97** *alt*. Ps. 74 Deut. 17. 8–end 1 Pet. 1. 13–end *or First EP of Philip and James* Ps. 25 Isa. 40. 27–end John 12. 20–26 **R ct**

May 2024

1 Wednesday **PHILIP AND JAMES, APOSTLES**

R	Isa. 30. 15–21 Ps. 119. 1–8 Eph. 1. 3–10 John 14. 1–14	*MP*: Ps. 139; 146 Prov. 4. 10–18 Jas. 1. 1–12	*EP*: Ps. 149 Job 23. 1–12 John 1. 43–end

May 2024			Sunday Principal Service Weekday Eucharist	Third Service Morning Prayer	Second Service Evening Prayer
2 Thursday	**Athanasius, Bishop of Alexandria, Teacher, 373**				
W	Com. Teacher *also* Ecclus. 4. 20–28 Matt. 10. 24–27	*or*	Acts 15. 7–21 Ps. 96. 1–3, 7–10 John 15. 9–11	Ps. ***57***; 148 *alt.* Ps. 78. 1–39† Num. 13. 1–3, 17–end Luke 5. 27–end	Ps. 104 *alt.* Ps. 78. 40–end† Deut. ch. 19 1 Pet. 2. 11–end
3 Friday					
W			Acts 15. 22–31 Ps. 57. 8–end John 15. 12–17	Ps. ***138***; 149 *alt.* Ps. 55 Num. 14. 1–25 Luke 6. 1–11	Ps. 66 *alt.* Ps. 69 Deut. 21.22 – 22.8 1 Pet. 3. 1–12
4 Saturday	**English Saints and Martyrs of the Reformation Era**				
W	Isa. 43. 1–7 *or* Ecclus. 2. 10–17 Ps. 87 2 Cor. 4. 5–12 John 12. 20–26	*or*	Acts 16. 1–10 Ps. 100 John 15. 18–21	Ps. ***146***; 150 *alt.* Ps. ***76***; 79 Num. 14. 26–end Luke 6. 12–26	Ps. 118 *alt.* Ps. 81; ***84*** Deut. 24. 5–end 1 Pet. 3. 13–end **ct**

5 Sunday	**THE SIXTH SUNDAY OF EASTER**			
W	*The reading from Acts must be used as either the first or second reading at the Principal Service.*	Acts 10. 44–end [Isa. 55. 1–11] Ps. 98 1 John 5. 1–6 John 15. 9–17	Ps. 104. 26–32 Ezek. 47. 1–12 John 21. 1–19	Ps. 45 Song of Sol. 4.16 – 5.2; 8. 6–7 Rev. 3. 14–end *Gospel*: Luke 22. 24–30
6 Monday	Rogation Day			
W		Acts 16. 11–15 Ps. 149. 1–5 John 15.26 – 16.4	Ps. ***65***; 67 *alt*. Ps. ***80***; 82 Num. 16. 1–35 Luke 6. 27–38	Ps. ***121***; 122; 123 *alt*. Ps. ***85***; 86 Deut. ch. 26 1 Pet. 4. 1–11
7 Tuesday	Rogation Day			
W		Acts 16. 22–34 Ps. 138 John 16. 5–11	Ps. 124; 125; ***126***; 127 *alt*. Ps. 87; ***89. 1–18*** Num. 16. 36–end Luke 6. 39–end	Ps. ***128***; 129; 130; 131 *alt*. Ps. 89. 19–end Deut. 28. 1–14 1 Pet. 4. 12–end

May 2024		Sunday Principal Service Weekday Eucharist	Third Service Morning Prayer	Second Service Evening Prayer
8 Wednesday	**Julian of Norwich, Spiritual Writer, *c.* 1417** Rogation Day			
W	Com. Religious *or* *also* 1 Cor. 13. 8–end Matt. 5. 13–16	Acts 17.15, 22 – 18.1 Ps. 148. 1–2, 11–end John 16. 12–15	Ps. ***132***; 133 *alt.* Ps. 119. 105–128 Num. 17. 1–11 Luke 7. 1–10	*First EP of Ascension Day* Ps. 15; 24 2 Sam. 23. 1–5 Col. 2.20 – 3.4 **𝔚 ct**
9 Thursday	**ASCENSION DAY**			
𝔚	*The reading from Acts must be used as either the first or second reading at the Eucharist.*	Acts 1. 1–11 *or* Dan. 7. 9–14 Ps. 47 *or* Ps. 93 Eph. 1. 15–end *or* Acts 1. 1–11 Luke 24. 44–end	*MP*: Ps. 110; 150 Isa. 52. 7–end Heb. 7. [11–25] 26–end	*EP*: Ps. 8 Song of the Three 29–37 *or* 2 Kings 2. 1–15 Rev. ch. 5 *Gospel*: Matt. 28. 16–end

10 Friday			
W	Acts 18. 9–18 Ps. 47. 1–6 John 16. 20–23	Ps. 20; ***81*** *alt.* Ps. ***88***; (95) Num. 20. 1–13 Luke 7. 11–17 [Exod. 35.30 - 36.1 Gal. 5. 13–end]*	Ps. 145 *alt.* Ps. 102 Deut. 29. 2–15 1 John 1.1 - 2.6
11 Saturday			
W	Acts 18. 22–end Ps. 47. 1–2, 7–end John 16. 23–28	Ps. 21; ***47*** *alt.* Ps. 96; ***97***; 100 Num. 21. 4–9 Luke 7. 18–35 [Num. 11. 16–17, 24–29 1 Cor. ch. 2]*	Ps. 84; ***85*** *alt.* Ps. 104 Deut. ch. 30 1 John 2. 7–17 **ct**

*The alternative readings in square brackets may be used at one of the offices, in preparation for the Day of Pentecost.

May 2024		Sunday Principal Service Weekday Eucharist	Third Service Morning Prayer	Second Service Evening Prayer
12 Sunday	**THE SEVENTH SUNDAY OF EASTER (SUNDAY AFTER ASCENSION DAY)**			
W	*The reading from Acts must be used as either the first or second reading at the Principal Service.*	Acts 1. 15–17, 21–end [Ezek. 36. 24–28] Ps. 1 1 John 5. 9–13 John 17. 6–19	Ps. 76 Isa. 14. 3–15 Rev. 14. 1–13	Ps. 147. 1–12 Isa. ch. 61 Luke 4. 14–21
13 Monday				
W		Acts 19. 1–8 Ps. 68. 1–6 John 16. 29–end	Ps. ***93***; 96; 97 *alt.* Ps. ***98***; 99; 101 Num. 22. 1–35 Luke 7. 36–end [Num. 27. 15–end 1 Cor. ch. 3]*	Ps. 18 *alt.* Ps. ***105***† (*or* 103) Deut. 31. 1–13 1 John 2. 18–end *or First EP of Matthias* Ps. 147 Isa. 22. 15–22 Phil. 3.13b – 4.1 **R ct**

14 Tuesday	**MATTHIAS THE APOSTLE***			
R		Isa. 22. 15–end *or* Acts 1. 15–end Ps. 15 Acts 1. 15–end *or* 1 Cor. 4. 1–7 John 15. 9–17	*MP*: Ps. 16; 147. 1–12 1 Sam. 2. 27–35 Acts 2. 37–end	*EP*: Ps. 80 1 Sam. 16. 1–13a Matt. 7. 15–27
	or, if Matthias is celebrated on 24 February:			
W		Acts 20. 17–27 Ps. 68. 9–10, 18–19 John 17. 1–11	Ps. 98; ***99***; 100 *alt.* Ps. ***106***† (*or* 103) Num. 22.36 – 23.12 Luke 8. 1–15 [1 Sam. 10. 1–10 1 Cor. 12. 1–13]*	Ps. 68 *alt.* Ps. 107† Deut. 31. 14–29 1 John 3. 1–10
15 Wednesday				
W		Acts 20. 28–end Ps. 68. 27–28, 32–end John 17. 11–19	Ps. 2; ***29*** *alt.* Ps. 110; ***111***; 112 Num. 23. 13–end Luke 8. 16–25 [1 Kings 19. 1–18 Matt. 3. 13–end]*	Ps. 36; ***46*** *alt.* Ps. 119. 129–152 Deut. 31.30 – 32.14 1 John 3. 11–end

*Matthias may be celebrated on 24 February instead of 14 May.

		Sunday Principal Service Weekday Eucharist	Third Service Morning Prayer	Second Service Evening Prayer
16 Thursday	*Caroline Chisholm, Social Reformer, 1877*			
W		Acts 22. 30; 23. 6–11 Ps. 16. 1, 5–end John 17. 20–end	Ps. ***24***; 72 *alt*. Ps. 113; ***115*** Num. ch. 24 Luke 8. 26–39 [Ezek. 11. 14–20 Matt. 9.35 – 10.20]*	Ps. 139 *alt*. Ps. 114; ***116***; 117 Deut. 32. 15–47 1 John 4. 1–6
17 Friday				
W		Acts 25. 13–21 Ps. 103. 1–2, 11–12, 19–20 John 21. 15–19	Ps. ***28***; 30 *alt*. Ps. 139 Num. 27. 12–end Luke 8. 40–end [Ezek. 36. 22–28 Matt. 12. 22–32]*	Ps. 147 *alt*. Ps. ***130***; 131; 137 Deut. ch. 33 1 John 4. 7–end

18 Saturday				
W		Acts 28. 16–20, 30–end Ps. 11. 4–end John 21. 20–end	Ps. 42; ***43*** *alt.* Ps. 120; ***121***; 122 Num. 32. 1–27 Luke 9. 1–17 [Mic. 3. 1–8 Eph. 6. 10–20]*	*First EP of Pentecost* Ps. 48 Deut. 16. 9–15 John 7. 37–39 **R ct**
19 Sunday	**DAY OF PENTECOST (Whit Sunday)**			
R	*The reading from Acts must be used as either the first or second reading at the Principal Service.*	Acts 2. 1–21 *or* Ezek. 37. 1–14 Ps. 104. 26–36, 37b (*or* 26–end) Rom. 8. 22–27 *or* Acts 2. 1–21 John 15. 26–27; 16. 4b–15	*MP*: Ps. 145 Isa. 11. 1–9 *or* Wisd. 7. 15–23 [24–27] 1 Cor. 12. 4–13	*EP*: Ps. 139. 1–11, 13–18, 23–24 (*or* 139. 1–11) Ezek. 36. 22–28 Acts 2. 22–38 *Gospel*: John 20. 19–23
20 Monday	**Alcuin of York, Deacon, Abbot of Tours, 804** Ordinary Time resumes today			
Gw **DEL 7**	Com. Religious *also* Col. 3. 12–16 John 4. 19–24 *or*	Jas. 3. 13–end Ps. 19. 7–end Mark 9. 14–29	Ps. 123; 124; 125; ***126*** Josh. ch. 1 Luke 9. 18–27	Ps. ***127***; 128; 129 Job ch. 1 Rom. 1. 1–17

*The alternative readings in square brackets may be used at one of the offices, in preparation for the Day of Pentecost.

May 2024		Sunday Principal Service Weekday Eucharist	Third Service Morning Prayer	Second Service Evening Prayer
21 Tuesday	*Helena, Protector of the Holy Places, 330*			
G		Jas. 4. 1–10 Ps. 55. 7–9, 24 Mark 9. 30–37	Ps. ***132***; 133 Josh. ch. 2 Luke 9. 28–36	Ps. (134); ***135*** Job ch. 2 Rom. 1. 18–end
22 Wednesday				
G		Jas. 4. 13–end Ps. 49. 1–2, 5–10 Mark 9. 38–40	Ps. 119. 153–end Josh. ch. 3 Luke 9. 37–50	Ps. 136 Job ch. 3 Rom. 2. 1–16
23 Thursday				
G		Jas. 5. 1–6 Ps. 49. 12–20 Mark 9. 41–end	Ps. ***143***; 146 Josh. 4.1 – 5.1 Luke 9. 51–end	Ps. ***138***; 140; 141 Job ch. 4 Rom. 2. 17–end
24 Friday	**John and Charles Wesley, Evangelists, Hymn Writers, 1791 and 1788**			
Gw	Com. Pastor *also* Eph. 5. 15–20 *or*	Jas. 5. 9–12 Ps. 103. 1–4, 8–13 Mark 10. 1–12	Ps. ***142***; 144 Josh. 5. 2–end Luke 10. 1–16	Ps. 145 Job ch. 5 Rom. 3. 1–20

25 Saturday	**The Venerable Bede, Monk at Jarrow, Scholar, Historian, 735** *Aldhelm, Bishop of Sherborne, 709*			
Gw	Com. Religious *also* Ecclus. 39. 1–10	*or* Jas. 5. 13–end Ps. 141. 1–4 Mark 10. 13–16	Ps. 147 Josh. 6. 1–20 Luke 10. 17–24	*First EP of Trinity Sunday* Ps. 97; 98 Isa. 40. 12–end Mark 1. 1–13 **𝔚 ct**
26 Sunday	**TRINITY SUNDAY**			
𝔚		Isa. 6. 1–8 Ps. 29 Rom. 8. 12–17 John 3. 1–17	*MP*: Ps. 33. 1–12 Prov. 8. 1–4, 22–31 2 Cor. 13. [5–10] 11–end	*EP*: Ps. 104. 1–10 Ezek. 1. 4–10, 22–28a Rev. ch. 4 *Gospel*: Mark 1. 1–13
27 Monday				
G **DEL 8**		1 Pet. 1. 3–9 Ps. 111 Mark 10. 17–27	Ps. ***1***: 2; 3 Josh. 7. 1–15 Luke 10. 25–37	Ps. **4**; 7 Job ch. 7 Rom. 4. 1–12
28 Tuesday	*Lanfranc, Prior of Le Bec, Archbishop of Canterbury, Scholar, 1089*			
G		1 Pet. 1. 10–16 Ps. 98. 1–5 Mark 10. 28–31	Ps. ***5***; 6; (8) Josh. 7. 16–end Luke 10. 38–end	Ps. **9**; 10† Job ch. 8 Rom. 4. 13–end

		Sunday Principal Service Weekday Eucharist	Third Service Morning Prayer	Second Service Evening Prayer
29 Wednesday				
G		1 Pet. 1. 18–end Ps. 147. 13–end Mark 10. 32–45	Ps. 119. 1–32 Josh. 8. 1–29 Luke 11. 1–13	Ps. ***11***; 12; 13 Job ch. 9 Rom. 5. 1–11 *or First EP of Corpus Christi* Ps. 110; 111 Exod. 16. 2–15 John 6. 22–35 **W ct**
30 Thursday	**DAY OF THANKSGIVING FOR HOLY COMMUNION (CORPUS CHRISTI)** **Josephine Butler, Social Reformer, 1906** *Joan of Arc, Visionary, 1431; Apolo Kivebulaya, Evangelist in Central Africa, 1933*			
W		Gen. 14. 18–20 Ps. 116. 10–end 1 Cor. 11. 23–26 John 6. 51–58	*MP*: Ps. 147 Deut. 8. 2–16 1 Cor. 10. 1–17	*EP*: Ps. 23; 42; 43 Prov. 9. 1–5 Luke 9. 11–17

	or, if Corpus Christi is not observed:			
Gw	Com. Saint *esp.* Isa. 58. 6–11 *also* 1 John 3. 18–23 Matt. 9. 10–13	*or* 1 Pet. 2. 2–5, 9–12 Ps. 100 Mark 10. 46–end	Ps. 14; ***15***; 16 Josh. 8. 30–end Luke 11. 14–28	Ps. 18† Job ch. 10 Rom. 5. 12–end *or First EP of the Visit of Mary to Elizabeth* Ps. 45 Song of Sol. 2. 8–14 Luke 1. 26–38 **W ct**
31 Friday	**THE VISIT OF THE BLESSED VIRGIN MARY TO ELIZABETH***			
W		Zeph. 3. 14–18 Ps. 113 Rom. 12. 9–16 Luke 1. 39–49 [50–56]	*MP*: Ps. 85; 150 1 Sam. 2. 1–10 Mark 3. 31–end	*EP*: Ps. 122; 127; 128 Zech. 2. 10–end John 3. 25–30
	or, if The Visitation is celebrated on 2 July:			
G		1 Pet. 4. 7–13 Ps. 96. 10–end Mark 11. 11–26	Ps. 17; ***19*** Josh. 9. 3–26 Luke 11. 29–36	Ps. 22 Job ch. 11 Rom. 6. 1–14

*The Visit of the Blessed Virgin Mary to Elizabeth may be celebrated on 2 July instead of 31 May.

June 2024

		Sunday Principal Service Weekday Eucharist	Third Service Morning Prayer	Second Service Evening Prayer
1 Saturday	**Justin, Martyr at Rome, *c.* 165**			
Gr	Com. Martyr *esp.* John 15. 18–21 *also* 1 Macc. 2. 15–22 1 Cor. 1. 18–25	*or* Jude 17, 20–end Ps. 63. 1–6 Mark 11. 27–end	Ps. 20; 21; ***23*** Josh. 10. 1–15 Luke 11. 37–end	Ps. ***24***; 25 Job ch. 12 Rom. 6. 15–end **ct**
2 Sunday	**THE FIRST SUNDAY AFTER TRINITY (Proper 4)**			
G	*Track 1* 1 Sam. 3. 1–10 [11–20] Ps. 139. 1–5, 12–18 2 Cor. 4. 5–12 Mark 2.23 – 3.6	*Track 2* Deut. 5. 12–15 Ps. 81. 1–10 2 Cor. 4. 5–12 Mark 2.23 – 3.6	Ps. 28; 32 Deut. 5. 1–21 Acts 21. 17–39a	Ps. 35 (*or* 35. 1–10) Jer. 5. 1–19 Rom. 7. 7–end *Gospel*: Luke 7. 1–10
3 Monday	*The Martyrs of Uganda, 1885–87 and 1977*			
G **DEL 9**		2 Pet. 1. 2–7 Ps. 91. 1–2, 14–end Mark 12. 1–12	Ps. 27; ***30*** Josh. ch. 14 Luke 12. 1–12	Ps. 26; ***28***; 29 Job ch. 13 Rom. 7. 1–6

4 Tuesday	*Petroc, Abbot of Padstow, 6th century*				
G			2 Pet. 3. 11–15a, 17–end Ps. 90. 1–4, 10, 14, 16 Mark 12. 13–17	Ps. 32; ***36*** Josh. 21.43 – 22.8 Luke 12. 13–21	Ps. 33 Job ch. 14 Rom. 7. 7–end
5 Wednesday	**Boniface (Wynfrith) of Crediton, Bishop, Apostle of Germany, Martyr, 754**				
Gr	Com. Martyr *also* Acts 20. 24–28	*or*	2 Tim. 1. 1–3, 6–12 Ps. 123 Mark 12. 18–27	Ps. 34 Josh. 22. 9–end Luke 12. 22–31	Ps. 119. 33–56 Job ch. 15 Rom. 8. 1–11
6 Thursday	*Ini Kopuria, Founder of the Melanesian Brotherhood, 1945*				
G			2 Tim. 2. 8–15 Ps. 25. 4–12 Mark 12. 28–34	Ps. 37† Josh. ch. 23 Luke 12. 32–40	Ps. 39; ***40*** Job 16.1 – 17.2 Rom. 8. 12–17
7 Friday					
G			2 Tim. 3. 10–end Ps. 119. 161–168 Mark 12. 35–37	Ps. 31 Josh. 24. 1–28 Luke 12. 41–48	Ps. 35 Job 17. 3–end Rom. 8. 18–30

		Sunday Principal Service Weekday Eucharist	Third Service Morning Prayer	Second Service Evening Prayer
8 Saturday	**Thomas Ken, Bishop of Bath and Wells, Nonjuror, Hymn Writer, 1711**			
Gw	Com. Bishop *esp.* 2 Cor. 4. 1–10 Matt. 24. 42–46	*or* 2 Tim. 4. 1–8 Ps. 71. 7–16 Mark 12. 38–end	Ps. 41; ***42***; 43 Josh. 24. 29–end Luke 12. 49–end	Ps. 45; ***46*** Job ch. 18 Rom. 8. 31–end **ct**
9 Sunday	**THE SECOND SUNDAY AFTER TRINITY (Proper 5)**			
G	*Track 1* 1 Sam. 8. 4–11 [12–15] 16–20; [11. 14–end] Ps. 138 2 Cor. 4.13 – 5.1 Mark 3. 20–end	*Track 2* Gen. 3. 8–15 Ps. 130 2 Cor. 4.13 – 5.1 Mark 3. 20–end	Ps. 36 Deut. 6. 10–end Acts 22.22 – 23.11	Ps. 37. 1–17 (*or* 37. 1–11) Jer. 6. 16–21 Rom. 9. 1–13 *Gospel*: Luke 7. 11–17

10 Monday			
G **DEL 10**	1 Kings 17. 1–6 Ps. 121 Matt. 5. 1–12	Ps. 44 Judg. ch. 2 Luke 13. 1–9	Ps. ***47***; 49 Job ch. 19 Rom. 9. 1–18 *or First EP of Barnabas* Ps. 1; 15 Isa. 42. 5–12 Acts 14. 8–end **R ct**
11 Tuesday **BARNABAS THE APOSTLE**			
R	Job 29. 11–16 *or* Acts 11. 19–end Ps. 112 Acts 11. 19–end *or* Gal. 2. 1–10 John 15. 12–17	*MP*: Ps. 100; 101; 117 Jer. 9. 23–24 Acts 4. 32–end	*EP*: Ps. 147 Eccles. 12. 9–end *or* Tobit 4. 5–11 Acts 9. 26–31
12 Wednesday			
G	1 Kings 18. 20–39 Ps. 16. 1, 6–end Matt. 5. 17–19	Ps. 119. 57–80 Judg. ch. 5 Luke 13. 22–end	Ps. ***59***; 60; (67) Job ch. 22 Rom. 10. 1–10

		Sunday Principal Service Weekday Eucharist	Third Service Morning Prayer	Second Service Evening Prayer
13 Thursday				
G		1 Kings 18. 41–end Ps. 65. 8–end Matt. 5. 20–26	Ps. 56; ***57***; (63†) Judg. 6. 1–24 Luke 14. 1–11	Ps. 61; ***62***; 64 Job ch. 23 Rom. 10. 11–end
14 Friday	*Richard Baxter, Puritan Divine, 1691*			
G		1 Kings 19. 9, 11–16 Ps. 27. 8–16 Matt. 5. 27–32	Ps. ***51***; 54 Judg. 6. 25–end Luke 14. 12–24	Ps. 38 Job ch. 24 Rom. 11. 1–12
15 Saturday	*Evelyn Underhill, Spiritual Writer, 1941*			
G		1 Kings 19. 19–end Ps. 16. 1–7 Matt. 5. 33–37	Ps. 68 Judg. ch. 7 Luke 14. 25–end	Ps. 65; ***66*** Job chs 25 & 26 Rom. 11. 13–24 **ct**

16 Sunday	THE THIRD SUNDAY AFTER TRINITY **(Proper 6)**			
G	*Track 1* 1 Sam. 15.34 – 16.13 Ps. 20 2 Cor. 5. 6–10 [11–13] 14–17 Mark 4. 26–34	*Track 2* Ezek. 17. 22–end Ps. 92. 1–4, 12–end (*or* 1–8) 2 Cor. 5. 6–10 [11–13] 14–17 Mark 4. 26–34	Ps. 42; 43 Deut. 10.12 – 11.1 Acts 23. 12–35	Ps. 39 Jer. 7. 1–16 Rom. 9. 14–26 *Gospel*: Luke 7.36 – 8.3
17 Monday	*Samuel and Henrietta Barnett, Social Reformers, 1913 and 1936*			
G **DEL 11**		1 Kings 21. 1–16 Ps. 5. 1–5 Matt. 5. 38–42	Ps. 71 Judg. 8. 22–end Luke 15. 1–10	Ps. **72**; 75 Job ch. 27 Rom. 11. 25–end
18 Tuesday	*Bernard Mizeki, Apostle of the MaShona, Martyr, 1896*			
G		1 Kings 21. 17–end Ps. 51. 1–9 Matt. 5. 43–end	Ps. 73 Judg. 9. 1–21 Luke 15. 11–end	Ps. 74 Job ch. 28 Rom. 12. 1–8
19 Wednesday	*Sundar Singh of India, Sadhu (holy man), Evangelist, Teacher, 1929*			
G		2 Kings 2. 1, 6–14 Ps. 31. 21–end Matt. 6. 1–6, 16–18	Ps. 77 Judg. 9. 22–end Luke 16. 1–18	Ps. 119. 81–104 Job ch. 29 Rom. 12. 9–end

June 2024		Sunday Principal Service Weekday Eucharist	Third Service Morning Prayer	Second Service Evening Prayer
20 Thursday				
G		Ecclus. 48. 1–14 *or* Isa. 63. 7–9 Ps. 97. 1–8 Matt. 6. 7–15	Ps. 78. 1–39† Judg. 11. 1–11 Luke 16. 19–end	Ps. 78. 40–end† Job ch. 30 Rom. 13. 1–7
21 Friday				
G		2 Kings 11. 1–4, 9–18, 20 Ps. 132. 1–5, 11–13 Matt. 6. 19–23	Ps. 55 Judg. 11. 29–end Luke 17. 1–10	Ps. 69 Job ch. 31 Rom. 13. 8–end
22 Saturday	**Alban, first Martyr of Britain, *c.* 250**			
Gr	Com. Martyr *esp.* 2 Tim. 2. 3–13 John 12. 24–26	*or* 2 Chron. 24. 17–25 Ps. 89. 25–33 Matt. 6. 24–end	Ps. ***76***; 79 Judg. 12. 1–7 Luke 17. 11–19	Ps. 81; ***84*** Job ch. 32 Rom. 14. 1–12 **ct**

23 Sunday	**THE FOURTH SUNDAY AFTER TRINITY (Proper 7)**			
G	*Track 1* 1 Sam. 17. [1a, 4–11, 19–23] 32–49 *and* Ps. 9. 9–end *or* 1 Sam. 17.57 - 18.5, 10–16 *and* Ps. 133 2 Cor. 6. 1–13 Mark 4. 35–end	*Track 2* Job 38. 1–11 Ps. 107. 1–3, 23–32 (*or* 23–32) 2 Cor. 6. 1–13 Mark 4. 35–end	Ps. 48 Deut. 11. 1–15 Acts 27. 1–12	Ps. 49 Jer. 10. 1–16 Rom. 11. 25–end *Gospel*: Luke 8. 26–39 *or First EP of The Birth of John the Baptist* Ps. 71 Judg. 13. 2–7, 24–end Luke 1. 5–25 **W ct**
24 Monday	**THE BIRTH OF JOHN THE BAPTIST**			
W **DEL 12**		Isa. 40. 1–11 Ps. 85. 7–end Acts 13. 14b–26 *or* Gal. 3. 23–end Luke 1. 57–66, 80	*MP*: Ps. 50; 149 Ecclus. 48. 1–10 *or* Mal. 3. 1–6 Luke 3. 1–17	*EP*: Ps. 80; 82 Mal. ch. 4 Matt. 11. 2–19
25 Tuesday				
G		2 Kings 19. 9b–11, 14–21, 31–36 Ps. 48. 1–2, 8–end Matt. 7. 6, 12–14	Ps. 87; ***89. 1–18*** Judg. ch. 14 Luke 18. 1–14	Ps. 89. 19–end Job ch. 38 Rom. 15. 1–13

June 2024		Sunday Principal Service Weekday Eucharist	Third Service Morning Prayer	Second Service Evening Prayer
26 Wednesday	Ember Day			
G *or* **R**		2 Kings 22. 8–13; 23. 1–3 Ps. 119. 33–40 Matt. 7. 15–20	Ps. 119. 105–128 Judg. 15.1 – 16.3 Luke 18. 15–30	Ps. ***91***; 93 Job ch. 39 Rom. 15. 14–21
27 Thursday	*Cyril, Bishop of Alexandria, Teacher, 444*			
G		2 Kings 24. 8–17 Ps. 79. 1–9, 12 Matt. 7. 21–end	Ps. 90; **92** Judg. 16. 4–end Luke 18. 31–end	Ps. 94 Job ch. 40 Rom. 15. 22–end
28 Friday	**Irenaeus, Bishop of Lyons, Teacher, *c.* 200** Ember Day			
Gw *or* **Rw**	Com. Teacher *also* 2 Pet. 1. 16–21 *or*	2 Kings 25. 1–12 Ps. 137. 1–6 Matt. 8. 1–4	Ps. ***88***; (95) Judg. ch. 17 Luke 19. 1–10	Ps. 102 Job ch. 41 Rom. 16. 1–16 *or First EP of Peter and Paul* Ps. 66; 67 Ezek. 3. 4–11 Gal. 1.13 – 2.8 *or, for Peter alone*: Acts 9. 32–end **R ct**

29 Saturday	**PETER AND PAUL, APOSTLES** Ember Day			
R		Zech. 4. 1–6a, 10b–end *or* Acts 12. 1–11 Ps. 125 Acts 12. 1–11 *or* 2 Tim. 4. 6–8, 17–18 Matt. 16. 13–19	*MP*: Ps. 71; 113 Isa. 49. 1–6 Acts 11. 1–18	*EP*: Ps. 124; 138 Ezek. 34. 11–16 John 21. 15–22
	or, if Peter is commemorated alone:			
R		Ezek. 3. 22–end *or* Acts 12. 1–11 Ps. 125 Acts 12. 1–11 *or* 1 Pet. 2. 19–end Matt. 16. 13–19	*MP*: Ps. 71; 113 Isa. 49. 1–6 Acts 11. 1–18	*EP*: Ps. 124; 138 Ezek. 34. 11–16 John 21. 15–22
30 Sunday	**THE FIFTH SUNDAY AFTER TRINITY (Proper 8)**			
G	*Track 1* 2 Sam. 1. 1, 17–end Ps. 130 2 Cor. 8. 7–end Mark 5. 21–end	*Track 2* Wisd. of Sol. 1. 13–15; 2. 23–24 *Canticle*: Lam. 3. 22–33 *or* Ps. 30 2 Cor. 8. 7–end Mark 5. 21–end	Ps. 56 Deut. 15. 1–11 Acts 27. [13–32] 33–end	Ps. [52]; 53 Jer. 11. 1–14 Rom. 13. 1–10 *Gospel*: Luke 9. 51–end

		Sunday Principal Service Weekday Eucharist	Third Service Morning Prayer	Second Service Evening Prayer
July 2024				
1 Monday	*Henry, John and Henry Venn the Younger, Priests, Evangelical Divines, 1797, 1813 and 1873*			
G **DEL 13**		Amos 2. 6–10, 13–end Ps. 50. 16–23 Matt. 8. 18–22	Ps. ***98***; 99; 101 1 Sam. 1. 1–20 Luke 19. 28–40	Ps. ***105***† (*or* 103) Ezek. 1. 1–14 2 Cor. 1. 1–14
2 Tuesday*				
G		Amos 3. 1–8; 4. 11–12 Ps. 5. 8–end Matt. 8. 23–27	Ps. ***106***† (*or* 103) 1 Sam. 1.21 – 2.11 Luke 19. 41–end	Ps. 107† Ezek. 1.15 – 2.2 2 Cor. 1.15 – 2.4 *or First EP of Thomas* Ps. 27 Isa. ch. 35 Heb. 10.35 – 11.1 **R ct**

3 Wednesday **THOMAS THE APOSTLE****

R	Hab. 2. 1–4 Ps. 31. 1–6 Eph. 2. 19–end John 20. 24–29	*MP*: Ps. 92; 146 2 Sam. 15. 17–21 *or* Ecclus. ch. 2 John 11. 1–16	*EP*: Ps. 139 Job 42. 1–6 1 Pet. 1. 3–12

or, if Thomas is not celebrated:

G	Amos 5. 14–15, 21–24 Ps. 50. 7–14 Matt. 8. 28–end	Ps. 110; ***111***; 112 1 Sam. 2. 12–26 Luke 20. 1–8	Ps. 119. 129–152 Ezek. 2.3 – 3.11 2 Cor. 2. 5–end

4 Thursday

G	Amos 7. 10–end Ps. 19. 7–10 Matt. 9. 1–8	Ps. 113; ***115*** 1 Sam. 2. 27–end Luke 20. 9–19	Ps. 114; ***116***; 117 Ezek. 3. 12–end 2 Cor. ch. 3

5 Friday

G	Amos 8. 4–6, 9–12 Ps. 119. 1–8 Matt. 9. 9–13	Ps. 139 1 Sam. 3.1 – 4.1a Luke 20. 20–26	Ps. ***130***; 131; 137 Ezek. ch. 8 2 Cor. ch. 4

*The Visit of the Blessed Virgin Mary to Elizabeth may be celebrated on 2 July instead of 31 May.
**Thomas the Apostle may be celebrated on 21 December instead of 3 July.

		Sunday Principal Service Weekday Eucharist	Third Service Morning Prayer	Second Service Evening Prayer
6 Saturday	*Thomas More, Scholar, and John Fisher, Bishop of Rochester, Reformation Martyrs, 1535*			
G		Amos 9. 11–end Ps. 85. 8–end Matt. 9. 14–17	Ps. 120; ***121***; 122 1 Sam. 4. 1b–end Luke 20. 27–40	Ps. 118 Ezek. ch. 9 2 Cor. ch. 5 **ct**
7 Sunday	**THE SIXTH SUNDAY AFTER TRINITY (Proper 9)**			
G	*Track 1* 2 Sam. 5. 1–5, 9–10 Ps. 48 2 Cor. 12. 2–10 Mark 6. 1–13	*Track 2* Ezek. 2. 1–5 Ps. 123 2 Cor. 12. 2–10 Mark 6. 1–13	Ps. 57 Deut. 24. 10–end Acts 28. 1–16	Ps. [63]; 64 Jer. 20. 1–11a Rom. 14. 1–17 *Gospel*: Luke 10. 1–11, 16–20
8 Monday				
G **DEL 14**		Hos. 2. 14–16, 19–20 Ps. 145. 2–9 Matt. 9. 18–26	Ps. 123; 124; 125; ***126*** 1 Sam. ch. 5 Luke 20.41 – 21.4	Ps. ***127***; 128; 129 Ezek. 10. 1–19 2 Cor. 6.1 – 7.1

9 Tuesday					
G			Hos. 8. 4-7, 11-13 Ps. 103. 8-12 Matt. 9. 32-end	Ps. ***132***; 133 1 Sam. 6. 1-16 Luke 21. 5-19	Ps. (134); ***135*** Ezek. 11. 14-end 2 Cor. 7. 2-end
10 Wednesday					
G			Hos. 10. 1-3, 7-8, 12 Ps. 115. 3-10 Matt. 10. 1-7	Ps. 119. 153-end 1 Sam. ch. 7 Luke 21. 20-28	Ps. 136 Ezek. 12. 1-16 2 Cor. 8. 1-15
11 Thursday	**Benedict of Nursia, Abbot of Monte Cassino, Father of Western Monasticism, c. 550**				
Gw	Com. Religious *also* 1 Cor. 3. 10-11 Luke 18. 18-22	*or*	Hos. 11. 1, 3-4, 8-9 Ps. 105. 1-7 Matt. 10. 7-15	Ps. ***143***; 146 1 Sam. ch. 8 Luke 21. 29-end	Ps. ***138***; 140; 141 Ezek. 12. 17-end 2 Cor. 8.16 - 9.5
12 Friday					
G			Hos. 14. 2-end Ps. 80. 1-7 Matt. 10. 16-23	Ps. 142; ***144*** 1 Sam. 9. 1-14 Luke 22. 1-13	Ps. 145 Ezek. 13. 1-16 2 Cor. 9. 6-end

July 2024		Sunday Principal Service Weekday Eucharist	Third Service Morning Prayer	Second Service Evening Prayer
13 Saturday				
G		Isa. 6. 1–8 Ps. 51. 1–7 Matt. 10. 24–33	Ps. 147 1 Sam. 9.15 – 10.1 Luke 22. 14–23	Ps. ***148***; 149; 150 Ezek. 14. 1–11 2 Cor. ch. 10 **ct**
14 Sunday	**THE SEVENTH SUNDAY AFTER TRINITY (Proper 10)**			
G	*Track 1* 2 Sam. 6. 1–5, 12b–19 Ps. 24 Eph. 1. 3–14 Mark 6. 14–29	*Track 2* Amos 7. 7–15 Ps. 85. 8–end Eph. 1. 3–14 Mark 6. 14–29	Ps. 65 Deut. 28. 1–14 Acts 28. 17–end	Ps. 66 (*or* 66. 1–8) Job 4. 1; 5. 6–end *or* Ecclus. 4. 11–end Rom. 15. 14–29 *Gospel*: Luke 10. 25–37
15 Monday	**Swithun, Bishop of Winchester, c. 862** *Bonaventure, Friar, Bishop, Teacher, 1274*			
Gw **DEL 15**	Com. Bishop *or* *also* Jas. 5. 7–11, 13–18	Isa. 1. 11–17 Ps. 50. 7–15 Matt. 10.34 – 11.1	Ps. ***1***; 2; 3 1 Sam. 10. 1–16 Luke 22. 24–30	Ps. ***4***; 7 Ezek. 14. 12–end 2 Cor. 11. 1–15

16 Tuesday	*Osmund, Bishop of Salisbury, 1099*				
G			Isa. 7. 1–9 Ps. 48. 1–7 Matt. 11. 20–24	Ps. ***5***; 6; (8) 1 Sam. 10. 17–end Luke 22. 31–38	Ps. ***9***; 10† Ezek. 18. 1–20 2 Cor. 11. 16–end
17 Wednesday					
G			Isa. 10. 5–7, 13–16 Ps. 94. 5–11 Matt. 11. 25–27	Ps. 119. 1–32 1 Sam. ch. 11 Luke 22. 39–46	Ps. ***11***; 12; 13 Ezek. 18. 21–32 2 Cor. ch. 12
18 Thursday	*Elizabeth Ferard, first Deaconess of the Church of England, Founder of the Community of St Andrew, 1883*				
G			Isa. 26. 7–9, 16–19 Ps. 102. 14–21 Matt. 11. 28–end	Ps. 14; ***15***; 16 1 Sam. ch. 12 Luke 22. 47–62	Ps. 18† Ezek. 20. 1–20 2 Cor. ch. 13
19 Friday	**Gregory, Bishop of Nyssa, and his sister Macrina, Deaconess, Teachers, *c.* 394 and *c.* 379**				
Gw	Com. Teacher *esp.* 1 Cor. 2. 9–13 *also* Wisd. 9. 13–17	*or*	Isa. 38. 1–6, 21–22, 7–8 *Canticle*: Isa. 38. 10–16 *or* Ps. 32. 1–8 Matt. 12. 1–8	Ps. 17; ***19*** 1 Sam. 13. 5–18 Luke 22. 63–end	Ps. 22 Ezek. 20. 21–38 Jas. 1. 1–11

		Sunday Principal Service Weekday Eucharist	Third Service Morning Prayer	Second Service Evening Prayer
20 Saturday	*Margaret of Antioch, Martyr, 4th century; Bartolomé de las Casas, Apostle to the Indies, 1566*			
G		Mic. 2. 1–5 Ps. 10. 1–5a, 12 Matt. 12. 14–21	Ps. 20; 21; ***23*** 1 Sam. 13.19 – 14.15 Luke 23. 1–12	Ps. ***24***; 25 Ezek. 24. 15–end Jas. 1. 12–end **ct**
21 Sunday	**THE EIGHTH SUNDAY AFTER TRINITY (Proper 11)**			
G	*Track 1* 2 Sam. 7. 1–14a Ps. 89. 20–37 Eph. 2. 11–end Mark 6. 30–34, 53–end	*Track 2* Jer. 23. 1–6 Ps. 23 Eph. 2. 11–end Mark 6. 30–34, 53–end	Ps. 67; 70 Deut. 30. 1–10 1 Pet. 3. 8–18	Ps. 73 (*or* 73. 21–end) Job 13.13 – 14.6 *or* Ecclus. 18. 1–14 Heb. 2. 5–end *Gospel*: Luke 10. 38–end *or First EP of Mary Magdalene* Ps. 139 Isa. 25. 1–9 2 Cor. 1. 3–7 **W ct**

22 Monday **MARY MAGDALENE**

W **DEL 16**	Song of Sol. 3. 1–4 Ps. 42. 1–10 2 Cor. 5. 14–17 John 20. 1–2, 11–18	*MP*: Ps. 30; 32; 150 1 Sam. 16. 14–end Luke 8. 1–3	*EP*: Ps. 63 Zeph. 3. 14–end Mark 15.40 – 16.7

23 Tuesday *Bridget of Sweden, Abbess of Vadstena, 1373*

G	Mic. 7. 14–15, 18–20 Ps. 85. 1–7 Matt. 12. 46–end	Ps. 32; ***36*** 1 Sam. 15. 1–23 Luke 23. 26–43	Ps. 33 Ezek. 33. 1–20 Jas. 2. 14–end

24 Wednesday

G	Jer. 1. 1, 4–10 Ps. 70 Matt. 13. 1–9	Ps. 34 1 Sam. ch. 16 Luke 23. 44–56a	Ps. 119. 33–56 Ezek. 33. 21–end Jas. ch. 3 *or First EP of James* Ps. 144 Deut. 30. 11–end Mark 5. 21–end **R ct**

July 2024		Sunday Principal Service Weekday Eucharist	Third Service Morning Prayer	Second Service Evening Prayer
25 Thursday	**JAMES THE APOSTLE**			
R		Jer. 45. 1–5 *or* Acts 11.27 – 12.2 Ps. 126 Acts 11.27 – 12.2 *or* 2 Cor. 4. 7–15 Matt. 20. 20–28	*MP*: Ps. 7; 29; 117 2 Kings 1. 9–15 Luke 9. 46–56	*EP*: Ps. 94 Jer. 26. 1–15 Mark 1. 14–20
26 Friday	**Anne and Joachim, Parents of the Blessed Virgin Mary**			
Gw	Zeph. 3. 14–18a Ps. 127 Rom. 8. 28–30 Matt. 13. 16–17 *or*	Jer. 3. 14–17 Ps. 23 *or Canticle*: Jer. 31. 10–13 Matt. 13. 18–23	Ps. 31 1 Sam. 17. 31–54 Luke 24. 13–35	Ps. 35 Ezek. 34. 17–end Jas. 4.13 – 5.6
27 Saturday	*Brooke Foss Westcott, Bishop of Durham, Teacher, 1901*			
G		Jer. 7. 1–11 Ps. 84. 1–6 Matt. 13. 24–30	Ps. 41; **42**; 43 1 Sam. 17.55 – 18.16 Luke 24. 36–end	Ps. 45; **46** Ezek. 36. 16–36 Jas. 5. 7–end **ct**

28 Sunday	THE NINTH SUNDAY AFTER TRINITY **(Proper 12)**				
G	*Track 1* 2 Sam. 11. 1–15 Ps. 14 Eph. 3. 14–end John 6. 1–21		*Track 2* 2 Kings 4. 42–end Ps. 145. 10–19 Eph. 3. 14–end John 6. 1–21	Ps. 75 Song of Sol. ch. 2 *or* 1 Macc. 2. [1–14] 15–22 1 Pet. 4. 7–14	Ps. 74 (*or* 74. 11–16) Job 19. 1–27a *or* Ecclus. 38. 24–end Heb. ch. 8 *Gospel*: Luke 11. 1–13
29 Monday	**Mary, Martha and Lazarus, Companions of Our Lord**				
Gw **DEL 17**	Isa. 25. 6–9 Ps. 49. 5–10, 16 Heb. 2. 10–15 John 12. 1–8	*or*	Jer. 13. 1–11 Ps. 82 *or* Deut. 32. 18–21 Matt. 13. 31–35	Ps. 44 1 Sam. 19. 1–18 Acts 1. 1–14	Ps. ***47***; 49 Ezek. 37. 1–14 Mark 1. 1–13
30 Tuesday	**William Wilberforce, Social Reformer, Olaudah Equiano and Thomas Clarkson, Anti-Slavery Campaigners, 1833, 1797 and 1846**				
Gw	Com. Saint *also* Job 31. 16–23 Gal. 3. 26–end; 4. 6–7 Luke 4. 16–21	*or*	Jer. 14. 17–end Ps. 79. 8–end Matt. 13. 36–43	Ps. ***48***; 52 1 Sam. 20. 1–17 Acts 1. 15–end	Ps. 50 Ezek. 37. 15–end Mark 1. 14–20

		Sunday Principal Service Weekday Eucharist	Third Service Morning Prayer	Second Service Evening Prayer
31 Wednesday	*Ignatius of Loyola, Founder of the Society of Jesus, 1556*			
G		Jer. 15. 10, 16–end Ps. 59. 1–4, 18–end Matt. 13. 44–46	Ps. 119. 57–80 1 Sam. 20. 18–end Acts 2. 1–21	Ps. ***59***; 60; (67) Ezek. 39. 21–end Mark 1. 21–28

August 2024

1 Thursday				
G		Jer. 18. 1–6 Ps. 146. 1–5 Matt. 13. 47–53	Ps. 56; ***57***; (63†) 1 Sam. 21.1 – 22.5 Acts 2. 22–36	Ps. 61; ***62***; 64 Ezek. 43. 1–12 Mark 1. 29–end
2 Friday				
G		Jer. 26. 1–9 Ps. 69. 4–10 Matt. 13. 54–end	Ps. ***51***; 54 1 Sam. 22. 6–end Acts 2. 37–end	Ps. 38 Ezek. 44. 4–16 Mark 2. 1–12

3 Saturday				
G		Jer. 26. 11-16, 24 Ps. 69. 14-20 Matt. 14. 1-12	Ps. 68 1 Sam. ch. 23 Acts 3. 1-10	Ps. 65; **66** Ezek. 47. 1-12 Mark 2. 13-22 **ct**
4 Sunday	**THE TENTH SUNDAY AFTER TRINITY (Proper 13)**			
G	*Track 1* 2 Sam. 11.26 – 12.13a Ps. 51. 1-13 Eph. 4. 1-16 John 6. 24-35	*Track 2* Exod. 16. 2-4, 9-15 Ps. 78. 23-29 Eph. 4. 1-16 John 6. 24-35	Ps. 86 Song of Sol. 5. 2-end *or* 1 Macc. 3. 1-12 2 Pet. 1. 1-15	Ps. 88 (*or* 88. 1-10) Job ch. 28 *or* Ecclus. 42. 15-end Heb. 11. 17-31 *Gospel*: Luke 12. 13-21
5 Monday	**Oswald, King of Northumbria, Martyr, 642**			
Gr **DEL 18**	Com. Martyr *or* *esp.* 1 Pet. 4. 12-end John 16. 29-end	Jer. ch. 28 Ps. 119. 89-96 Matt. 14. 13-21 *or* 14. 22-end	Ps. 71 1 Sam. ch. 24 Acts 3. 11-end	Ps. **72**; 75 Prov. 1. 1-19 Mark 2.23 – 3.6 *or First EP of The Transfiguration* Ps. 99; 110 Exod. 24. 12-end John 12. 27-36a **𝔚 ct**

August 2024		Sunday Principal Service Weekday Eucharist	Third Service Morning Prayer	Second Service Evening Prayer
6 Tuesday	**THE TRANSFIGURATION OF OUR LORD**			
𝔚		Dan. 7. 9–10, 13–14 Ps. 97 2 Pet. 1. 16–19 Luke 9. 28–36	*MP*: Ps. 27; 150 Ecclus. 48. 1–10 *or* 1 Kings 19. 1–16 1 John 3. 1–3	*EP*: Ps. 72 Exod. 34. 29–end 2 Cor. ch. 3
7 Wednesday	*John Mason Neale, Priest, Hymn Writer, 1866*			
G		Jer. 31. 1–7 Ps. 121 Matt. 15. 21–28	Ps. 77 1 Sam. 28. 3–end Acts 4. 13–31	Ps. 119. 81–104 Prov. ch. 2 Mark 3. 19b–end
8 Thursday	**Dominic, Priest, Founder of the Order of Preachers, 1221**			
Gw	Com. Religious *or* *also* Ecclus. 39. 1–10	Jer. 31. 31–34 Ps. 51. 11–18 Matt. 16. 13–23	Ps. 78. 1–39† 1 Sam. ch. 31 Acts 4.32 – 5.11	Ps. 78. 40–end† Prov. 3. 1–26 Mark 4. 1–20

9 Friday	**Mary Sumner, Founder of the Mothers' Union, 1921**				
Gw	Com. Saint *also* Heb. 13. 1–5	*or*	Nahum 2. 1, 3; 3. 1–3, 6–7 Ps. 137. 1–6 *or* Deut. 32. 35–36, 39, 41 Matt. 16. 24–28	Ps. 55 2 Sam. ch. 1 Acts 5. 12–26	Ps. 69 Prov. 3.27 – 4.19 Mark 4. 21–34
10 Saturday	**Laurence, Deacon at Rome, Martyr, 258**				
Gr	Com. Martyr *also* 2 Cor. 9. 6–10	*or*	Hab. 1.12 – 2.4 Ps. 9. 7–11 Matt. 17. 14–20	Ps. ***76***; 79 2 Sam. 2. 1–11 Acts 5. 27–end	Ps. 81; ***84*** Prov. 6. 1–19 Mark 4. 35–end **ct**
11 Sunday	**THE ELEVENTH SUNDAY AFTER TRINITY (Proper 14)**				
G	*Track 1* 2 Sam. 18. 5–9, 15, 31–33 Ps. 130 Eph. 4.25 – 5.2 John 6. 35, 41–51		*Track 2* 1 Kings 19. 4–8 Ps. 34. 1–8 Eph. 4.25 – 5.2 John 6. 35, 41–51	Ps. 90 Song of Sol. 8. 5–7 *or* 1 Macc. 14. 4–15 2 Pet. 3. 8–13	Ps. 91 (*or* 91. 1–12) Job 39.1 – 40.4 *or* Ecclus. 43. 13–end Heb. 12. 1–17 *Gospel*: Luke 12. 32–40
12 Monday					
G **DEL 19**			Ezek. 1. 2–5, 24–end Ps. 148. 1–4, 12–13 Matt. 17. 22–end	Ps. ***80***; 82 2 Sam. 3. 12–end Acts ch. 6	Ps. ***85***; 86 Prov. 8. 1–21 Mark 5. 1–20

		Sunday Principal Service Weekday Eucharist	Third Service Morning Prayer	Second Service Evening Prayer
13 Tuesday	**Jeremy Taylor, Bishop of Down and Connor, Teacher, 1667** *Florence Nightingale, Nurse, Social Reformer, 1910; Octavia Hill, Social Reformer, 1912*			
Gw	Com. Teacher *also* Titus 2. 7–8, 11–14 *or*	Ezek. 2.8 – 3.4 Ps. 119. 65–72 Matt. 18. 1–5, 10, 12–14	Ps. 87; ***89. 1–18*** 2 Sam. 5. 1–12 Acts 7. 1–16	Ps. 89. 19–end Prov. 8. 22–end Mark 5. 21–34
14 Wednesday	*Maximilian Kolbe, Friar, Martyr, 1941*			
G		Ezek. 9. 1–7; 10. 18–22 Ps. 113 Matt. 18. 15–20	Ps. 119. 105–128 2 Sam. 6. 1–19 Acts 7. 17–43	Ps. ***91***; 93 Prov. ch. 9 Mark 5. 35–end *or First EP of The Blessed Virgin Mary* Ps. 72 Prov. 8. 22–31 John 19. 23–27 **W ct**

15 Thursday **THE BLESSED VIRGIN MARY***

	Principal Service	Morning	Evening
W	Isa. 61. 10–end *or* Rev. 11.19 – 12.6, 10 Ps. 45. 10–end Gal. 4. 4–7 Luke 1. 46–55	*MP*: Ps. 98; 138; 147. 1–12 Isa. 7. 10–15 Luke 11. 27–28	*EP*: Ps. 132 Song of Sol. 2. 1–7 Acts 1. 6–14

or, if The Blessed Virgin Mary is celebrated on 8 September:

G	Ezek. 12. 1–12 Ps. 78. 58–64 Matt. 18.21 – 19.1	Ps. 90; **92** 2 Sam. 7. 1–17 Acts 7. 44–53	Ps. 94 Prov. 10. 1–12 Mark 6. 1–13

16 Friday

G	Ezek. 16. 1–15, 60–end Ps. 118. 14–18 *or Canticle*: Song of Deliverance Matt. 19. 3–12	Ps. ***88***; (95) 2 Sam. 7. 18–end Acts 7.54 – 8.3	Ps. 102 Prov. 11. 1–12 Mark 6. 14–29

*The Blessed Virgin Mary may be celebrated on 8 September instead of 15 August.

August 2024		Sunday Principal Service Weekday Eucharist	Third Service Morning Prayer	Second Service Evening Prayer
17 Saturday				
G		Ezek. 18. 1–11a, 13b, 30, 32 Ps. 51. 1–3, 15–17 Matt. 19. 13–15	Ps. 96; **97**; 100 2 Sam. ch. 9 Acts 8. 4–25	Ps. 104 Prov. 12. 10–end Mark 6. 30–44 **ct**
18 Sunday	**THE TWELFTH SUNDAY AFTER TRINITY (Proper 15)**			
G	*Track 1* 1 Kings 2. 10–12; 3. 3–14 Ps. 111 Eph. 5. 15–20 John 6. 51–58	*Track 2* Prov. 9. 1–6 Ps. 34. 9–14 Eph. 5. 15–20 John 6. 51–58	Ps. 106. 1–10 Jonah ch. 1 *or* Ecclus. 3. 1–15 2 Pet. 3. 14–end	Ps. [92]; 100 Exod. 2.23 – 3.10 Heb. 13. 1–15 *Gospel*: Luke 12. 49–56
19 Monday				
G **DEL 20**		Ezek. 24. 15–24 Ps. 78. 1–8 Matt. 19. 16–22	Ps. **98**; 99; 101 2 Sam. ch. 11 Acts 8. 26–end	Ps. ***105***† (*or* 103) Prov. 14.31 – 15.17 Mark 6. 45–end

20 Tuesday	**Bernard, Abbot of Clairvaux, Teacher, 1153** *William and Catherine Booth, Founders of the Salvation Army, 1912 and 1890*				
Gw	Com. Religious *esp.* Rev. 19. 5–9	*or*	Ezek. 28. 1–10 Ps. 107. 1–3, 40, 43 Matt. 19. 23–end	Ps. ***106***† (*or* 103) 2 Sam. 12. 1–25 Acts 9. 1–19a	Ps. 107† Prov. 15. 18–end Mark 7. 1–13
21 Wednesday					
G			Ezek. 34. 1–11 Ps. 23 Matt. 20. 1–16	Ps. 110; ***111***; 112 2 Sam. 15. 1–12 Acts 9. 19b–31	Ps. 119. 129–152 Prov. 18. 10–end Mark 7. 14–23
22 Thursday					
G			Ezek. 36. 23–28 Ps. 51. 7–12 Matt. 22. 1–14	Ps. 113; ***115*** 2 Sam. 15. 13–end Acts 9. 32–end	Ps. 114; ***116***; 117 Prov. 20. 1–22 Mark 7. 24–30

August 2024		Sunday Principal Service Weekday Eucharist	Third Service Morning Prayer	Second Service Evening Prayer
23 Friday				
G		Ezek. 37. 1–14 Ps. 107. 1–8 Matt. 22. 34–40	Ps. 139 2 Sam. 16. 1–14 Acts 10. 1–16	Ps. ***130***; 131; 137 Prov. 22. 1–16 Mark 7. 31–end *or First EP of Bartholomew* Ps. 97 Isa. 61. 1–9 2 Cor. 6. 1–10 **R ct**
24 Saturday	**BARTHOLOMEW THE APOSTLE**			
R		Isa. 43. 8–13 *or* Acts 5. 12–16 Ps. 145. 1–7 Acts 5. 12–16 *or* 1 Cor. 4. 9–15 Luke 22. 24–30	*MP*: Ps. 86; 117 Gen. 28. 10–17 John 1. 43–end	*EP*: Ps. 91; 116 Ecclus. 39. 1–10 *or* Deut. 18. 15–19 Matt. 10. 1–22

25 Sunday	**THE THIRTEENTH SUNDAY AFTER TRINITY (Proper 16)**				
G	*Track 1* 1 Kings 8. [1, 6, 10–11] 22–30, 41–43 Ps. 84 Eph. 6. 10–20 John 6. 56–69		*Track 2* Josh. 24. 1–2a, 14–18 Ps. 34. 15–end Eph. 6. 10–20 John 6. 56–69	Ps. 115 Jonah ch. 2 *or* Ecclus. 3. 17–29 Rev. ch. 1	Ps. 116 (*or* 116. 10–end) Exod. 4.27 – 5.1 Heb. 13. 16–21 *Gospel*: Luke 13. 10–17
26 Monday					
G **DEL 21**			2 Thess. 1. 1–5, 11–end Ps. 39. 1–9 Matt. 23. 13–22	Ps. 123; 124; 125; ***126*** 2 Sam. 18. 1–18 Acts 10. 34–end	Ps. ***127***; 128; 129 Prov. 25. 1–14 Mark 8. 11–21
27 Tuesday	**Monica, Mother of Augustine of Hippo, 387**				
Gw	Com. Saint *also* Ecclus. 26. 1–3, 13–16	*or*	2 Thess. 2. 1–3a, 14–end Ps. 98 Matt. 23. 23–26	Ps. ***132***; 133 2 Sam. 18.19 – 19.8a Acts 11. 1–18	Ps. (134); ***135*** Prov. 25. 15–end Mark 8. 22–26
28 Wednesday	**Augustine, Bishop of Hippo, Teacher, 430**				
Gw	Com. Teacher *esp.* Ecclus. 39. 1–10 *also* Rom. 13. 11–13	*or*	2 Thess. 3. 6–10, 16–end Ps. 128 Matt. 23. 27–32	Ps. 119. 153–end 2 Sam. 19. 8b–23 Acts 11. 19–end	Ps. 136 Prov. 26. 12–end Mark 8.27 – 9.1

August/ September 2024			Sunday Principal Service Weekday Eucharist	Third Service Morning Prayer	Second Service Evening Prayer
29 Thursday	**The Beheading of John the Baptist**				
Gr	Jer. 1. 4–10 Ps. 11 Heb. 11.32 – 12.2 Matt. 14. 1–12	*or*	1 Cor. 1. 1–9 Ps. 145. 1–7 Matt. 24. 42–end	Ps. ***143***; 146 2 Sam. 19. 24–end Acts 12. 1–17	Ps. ***138***; 140; 141 Prov. 27. 1–22 Mark 9. 2–13
30 Friday	**John Bunyan, Spiritual Writer, 1688**				
Gw	Com. Teacher *also* Heb. 12. 1–2 Luke 21. 21, 34–36	*or*	1 Cor. 1. 17–25 Ps. 33. 6–12 Matt. 25. 1–13	Ps. 142; ***144*** 2 Sam. 23. 1–7 Acts 12. 18–end	Ps. 145 Prov. 30. 1–9, 24–31 Mark 9. 14–29
31 Saturday	**Aidan, Bishop of Lindisfarne, Missionary, 651**				
Gw	Com. Missionary *also* 1 Cor. 9. 16–19	*or*	1 Cor. 1. 26–end Ps. 33. 12–15, 20–end Matt. 25. 14–30	Ps. 147 2 Sam. ch. 24 Acts 13. 1–12	Ps. ***148***; 149; 150 Prov. 31. 10–end Mark 9. 30–37 **ct**

September 2024

1 Sunday	**THE FOURTEENTH SUNDAY AFTER TRINITY (Proper 17)**			
G	*Track 1* Song of Sol. 2. 8–13 Ps. 45. 1–2, 6–9 (*or* 1–7) Jas. 1. 17–end Mark 7. 1–8, 14–15, 21–23	*Track 2* Deut. 4. 1–2, 6–9 Ps. 15 Jas. 1. 17–end Mark 7. 1–8, 14–15, 21–23	Ps. 119. 17–40 Jonah 3. 1–9 *or* Ecclus. 11. 7–28 (*or* 19–28) Rev. 3. 14–end	Ps. 119. 1–16 (*or* 9–16) Exod. 12. 21–27 Matt. 4.23 – 5.20
2 Monday	*The Martyrs of Papua New Guinea, 1901 and 1942*			
G **DEL 22**		1 Cor. 2. 1–5 Ps. 33. 12–21 Luke 4. 16–30	Ps. ***1***; 2; 3 1 Kings 1. 5–31 Acts 13. 13–43	Ps. ***4***; 7 Wisd. ch. 1 *or* 1 Chron. 10.1 – 11.9 Mark 9. 38–end
3 Tuesday	**Gregory the Great, Bishop of Rome, Teacher, 604**			
Gw	Com. Teacher *also* 1 Thess. 2. 3–8	*or* 1 Cor. 2. 10b–end Ps. 145. 10–17 Luke 4. 31–37	Ps. ***5***; 6; (8) 1 Kings 1.32 – 2.4, 10–12 Acts 13.44 – 14.7	Ps. ***9***; 10† Wisd. ch. 2 *or* 1 Chron. ch. 13 Mark 10. 1–16

September 2024		Sunday Principal Service Weekday Eucharist	Third Service Morning Prayer	Second Service Evening Prayer
4 Wednesday	*Birinus, Bishop of Dorchester (Oxon), Apostle of Wessex, 650**			
G		1 Cor. 3. 1–9 Ps. 62 Luke 4. 38–end	Ps. 119. 1–32 1 Kings ch. 3 Acts 14. 8–end	Ps. ***11***; 12; 13 Wisd. 3. 1–9 *or* 1 Chron. 15.1 – 16.3 Mark 10. 17–31
5 Thursday				
G		1 Cor. 3. 18–end Ps. 24. 1–6 Luke 5. 1–11	Ps. 14; ***15***; 16 1 Kings 4.29 – 5.12 Acts 15. 1–21	Ps. 18† Wisd. 4. 7–end *or* 1 Chron. ch. 17 Mark 10. 32–34
6 Friday	*Allen Gardiner, Founder of the South American Mission Society, 1851*			
G		1 Cor. 4. 1–5 Ps. 37. 3–8 Luke 5. 33–end	Ps. 17; ***19*** 1 Kings 6. 1, 11–28 Acts 15. 22–35	Ps. 22 Wisd. 5. 1–16 *or* 1 Chron. 21.1 – 22.1 Mark 10. 35–45

7 Saturday				
G		1 Cor. 4. 6–15 Ps. 145. 18–end Luke 6. 1–5	Ps. 20; 21; ***23*** 1 Kings 8. 1–30 Acts 15.36 – 16.5	Ps. ***24***; 25 Wisd. 5.17 – 6.11 *or* 1 Chron. 22. 2–end Mark 10. 46–end **ct**
8 Sunday	**THE FIFTEENTH SUNDAY AFTER TRINITY (Proper 18)**** (The Accession of King Charles III may be observed on 8 September, and Collect, Readings and Post-Communion for the sovereign used.)			
G	*Track 1* Prov. 22. 1–2, 8–9, 22–23 Ps. 125 Jas. 2. 1–10 [11–13] 14–17 Mark 7. 24–end	*Track 2* Isa. 35. 4–7a Ps. 146 Jas. 2. 1–10 [11–13] 14–17 Mark 7. 24–end	Ps. 119. 57–72 Jonah 3.10 – 4.11 *or* Ecclus. 27.30 – 28.9 Rev. 8. 1–5	Ps. 119. 41–56 (*or* 49–56) Exod. 14. 5–end Matt. 6. 1–18
9 Monday	*Charles Fuge Lowder, Priest, 1880*			
G **DEL 23**		1 Cor. 5. 1–8 Ps. 5. 5–9a Luke 6. 6–11	Ps. 27; ***30*** 1 Kings 8. 31–62 Acts 16. 6–24	Ps. 26; ***28***; 29 Wisd. 6. 12–23 *or* 1 Chron. 28. 1–10 Mark 11. 1–11

*Cuthbert may be celebrated on 4 September instead of 20 March.
**The Blessed Virgin Mary may be celebrated on 8 September instead of 15 August.

September 2024		Sunday Principal Service Weekday Eucharist	Third Service Morning Prayer	Second Service Evening Prayer
10 Tuesday				
G		1 Cor. 6. 1–11 Ps. 149. 1–5 Luke 6. 12–19	Ps. 32; ***36*** 1 Kings 8.63 – 9.9 Acts 16. 25–end	Ps. 33 Wisd. 7. 1–14 *or* 1 Chron. 28. 11–end Mark 11. 12–26
11 Wednesday				
G		1 Cor. 7. 25–31 Ps. 45. 11–end Luke 6. 20–26	Ps. 34 1 Kings 10. 1–25 Acts 17. 1–15	Ps. 119. 33–56 Wisd. 7.15 – 8.4 *or* 1 Chron. 29. 1–9 Mark 11. 27–end
12 Thursday				
G		1 Cor. 8. 1–7, 11–end Ps. 139. 1–9 Luke 6. 27–38	Ps. 37† 1 Kings 11. 1–13 Acts 17. 16–end	Ps. 39; ***40*** Wisd. 8. 5–18 *or* 1 Chron. 29. 10–20 Mark 12. 1–12

13 Friday	**John Chrysostom, Bishop of Constantinople, Teacher, 407**			
Gw	Com. Teacher *esp.* Matt. 5. 13–19 *also* Jer. 1. 4–10	*or* 1 Cor. 9. 16–19, 22–end Ps. 84. 1–6 Luke 6. 39–42	Ps. 31 1 Kings 11. 26–end Acts 18. 1–21	Ps. 35 Wisd. 8.21 – 9.end *or* 1 Chron. 29. 21–end Mark 12. 13–17 *or First EP of Holy Cross Day* Ps. 66 Isa, 52.13 – 53.end Eph. 2. 11–end **R ct**
14 Saturday	**HOLY CROSS DAY**			
R		Num. 21. 4–9 Ps. 22. 23–28 Phil. 2. 6–11 John 3. 13–17	*MP*: Ps. 2; 8; 146 Gen. 3. 1–15 John 12. 27–36a	*EP*: Ps. 110; 150 Isa. 63. 1–16 1 Cor. 1. 18–25
15 Sunday	**THE SIXTEENTH SUNDAY AFTER TRINITY (Proper 19)**			
G	*Track 1* Prov. 1. 20–33 Ps. 19 (*or* 19. 1–6) *or Canticle*: Wisd. 7.26 – 8.1 Jas. 3. 1–12 Mark 8. 27–end	*Track 2* Isa. 50. 4–9a Ps. 116. 1–8 Jas. 3. 1–12 Mark 8. 27–end	Ps. 119. 105–120 Isa. 44.24 – 45.8 Rev. 12. 1–12	Ps. 119. 73–88 (*or* 73–80) Exod. 18. 13–26 Matt. 7. 1–14

September 2024			Sunday Principal Service Weekday Eucharist	Third Service Morning Prayer	Second Service Evening Prayer
16 Monday	**Ninian, Bishop of Galloway, Apostle of the Picts, c. 432** *Edward Bouverie Pusey, Priest, Tractarian, 1882*				
Gw **DEL 24**	Com. Missionary *esp.* Acts 13. 46–49 Mark 16. 15–end	*or*	1 Cor. 11. 17–26, 33 Ps. 40. 7–11 Luke 7. 1–10	Ps. 44 1 Kings 12.25 – 13.10 Acts 19. 8–20	Ps. ***47***; 49 Wisd. 11.21 – 12.2 *or* 2 Chron. 2. 1–16 Mark 12. 28–34
17 Tuesday	**Hildegard, Abbess of Bingen, Visionary, 1179**				
Gw	Com. Religious *also* 1 Cor. 2. 9–13 Luke 10. 21–24	*or*	1 Cor. 12. 12–14, 27–end Ps. 100 Luke 7. 11–17	Ps. ***48***; 52 1 Kings 13. 11–end Acts 19. 21–end	Ps. 50 Wisd. 12. 12–21 *or* 2 Chron. ch. 3 Mark 12. 35–end
18 Wednesday					
G			1 Cor. 12.13b – 13.end Ps. 33. 1–12 Luke 7. 31–35	Ps. 119. 57–80 1 Kings ch. 17 Acts 20. 1–16	Ps. ***59***; 60; (67) Wisd. 13. 1–9 *or* 2 Chron. ch. 5 Mark 13. 1–13

19 Thursday	*Theodore of Tarsus, Archbishop of Canterbury, 690*				
G			1 Cor. 15. 1–11 Ps. 118. 1–2, 17–20 Luke 7. 36–end	Ps. 56; ***57***; (63†) 1 Kings 18. 1–20 Acts 20. 17–end	Ps. 61; ***62***; 64 Wisd. 16.15 – 17.1 *or* 2 Chron. 6. 1–21 Mark 13. 14–23
20 Friday	**John Coleridge Patteson, first Bishop of Melanesia, and his Companions, Martyrs, 1871**				
Gr	Com. Martyr *esp.* 2 Chron. 24. 17–21 *also* Acts 7. 55–end	*or*	1 Cor. 15. 12–20 Ps. 17. 1–8 Luke 8. 1–3	Ps. ***51***; 54 1 Kings 18. 21–end Acts 21. 1–16	Ps. 38 Wisd. 18. 6–19 *or* 2 Chron. 6. 22–end Mark 13. 24–31 *or First EP of Matthew* Ps. 34 Isa. 33. 13–17 Matt. 6. 19–end **R ct**
21 Saturday	**MATTHEW, APOSTLE AND EVANGELIST**				
R			Prov. 3. 13–18 Ps. 119. 65–72 2 Cor. 4. 1–6 Matt. 9. 9–13	*MP*: Ps. 49; 117 1 Kings 19. 15–end 2 Tim. 3. 14–end	*EP*: Ps. 119. 33–40, 89–96 Eccles. 5. 4–12 Matt. 19. 16–end

September 2024		Sunday Principal Service Weekday Eucharist	Third Service Morning Prayer	Second Service Evening Prayer
22 Sunday	**THE SEVENTEENTH SUNDAY AFTER TRINITY (Proper 20)**			
G	*Track 1* Prov. 31. 10–end Ps. 1 Jas. 3.13 – 4.3, 7–8a Mark 9. 30–37	*Track 2* Wisd. 1.16 – 2.1, 12–22 *or* Jer. 11. 18–20 Ps. 54 Jas. 3.13 – 4.3, 7–8a Mark 9. 30–37	Ps. 119. 153–end Isa. 45. 9–22 Rev. 14. 1–5	Ps. 119. 137–152 (*or* 137–144) Exod. 19. 10–end Matt. 8. 23–end
23 Monday				
G **DEL 25**		Prov. 3. 27–34 Ps. 15 Luke 8. 16–18	Ps. 71 1 Kings ch. 21 Acts 21.37 – 22.21	Ps. **72**; 75 1 Macc. 1. 1–19 *or* 2 Chron. 9. 1–12 Mark 14. 1–11
24 Tuesday				
G		Prov. 21. 1–6, 10–13 Ps. 119. 1–8 Luke 8. 19–21	Ps. 73 1 Kings 22. 1–28 Acts 22.22 – 23.11	Ps. 74 1 Macc. 1. 20–40 *or* 2 Chron. 10.1 – 11.4 Mark 14. 12–25

25 Wednesday **Lancelot Andrewes, Bishop of Winchester, Spiritual Writer, 1626**
Ember Day
Sergei of Radonezh, Russian Monastic Reformer, Teacher, 1392

Gw *or* **Rw**	Com. Bishop *esp.* Isa. 6. 1–8	*or*	Prov. 30. 5–9 Ps. 119. 105–112 Luke 9. 1–6	Ps. 77 1 Kings 22. 29–45 Acts 23. 12–end	Ps. 119. 81–104 1 Macc. 1. 41–end *or* 2 Chron. ch. 12 Mark 14. 26–42

26 Thursday *Wilson Carlile, Founder of the Church Army, 1942*

G			Eccles. 1. 2–11 Ps. 90. 1–6 Luke 9. 7–9	Ps. 78. 1–39† 2 Kings 1. 2–17 Acts 24. 1–23	Ps. 78. 40–end† 1 Macc. 2. 1–28 *or* 2 Chron. 13.1 – 14.1 Mark 14. 43–52

27 Friday **Vincent de Paul, Founder of the Congregation of the Mission (Lazarists), 1660**
Ember Day

Gw *or* **Rw**	Com. Religious *also* 1 Cor. 1. 25–end Matt. 25. 34–40	*or*	Eccles. 3. 1–11 Ps. 144. 1–4 Luke 9. 18–22	Ps. 55 2 Kings 2. 1–18 Acts 24.24 – 25.12	Ps. 69 1 Macc. 2. 29–48 *or* 2 Chron. 14. 2–end Mark 14. 53–65

September/ October 2024		Sunday Principal Service Weekday Eucharist	Third Service Morning Prayer	Second Service Evening Prayer
28 Saturday	Ember Day			
G *or* **R**		Eccles. 11.9 – 12.8 Ps. 90. 1–2, 12–end Luke 9. 43b–45	Ps. ***76***; 79 2 Kings 4. 1–37 Acts 25. 13–end	Ps. 81; ***84*** 1 Macc. 2. 49–end *or* 2 Chron. 15. 1–15 Mark 14. 66–end *or First EP of Michael and All Angels* Ps. 91 2 Kings 6. 8–17 Matt. 18. 1–6, 10 **W ct**
29 Sunday	**MICHAEL AND ALL ANGELS** (*or transferred to 30 September*) or **THE EIGHTEENTH SUNDAY AFTER TRINITY (Proper 21)**			
W		Gen. 28. 10–17 *or* Rev. 12. 7–12 Ps. 103. 19–end Rev. 12. 7–12 *or* Heb. 1. 5–end John 1. 47–end	*MP*: Ps. 34; 150 Tobit 12. 6–end *or* Dan. 12. 1–4 Acts 12. 1–11	*EP*: Ps. 138; 148 Dan. 10. 4–end Rev. ch. 5

	or, for The Eighteenth Sunday after Trinity (Proper 21):			
G	*Track 1* Esth. 7. 1–6, 9–10; 9. 20–22 Ps. 124 Jas. 5. 13–end Mark 9. 38–end	*Track 2* Num. 11. 4–6, 10–16, 24–29 Ps. 19. 7–end Jas. 5. 13–end Mark 9. 38–end	Ps. 122 Isa. 48. 12–end Luke 11. 37–end	Ps. 120; 121 Exod. ch. 24 Matt. 9. 1–8

30 Monday — *Jerome, Translator of the Scriptures, Teacher, 420*

G **DEL 26**	Job 1. 6–end Ps. 17. 1–11 Luke 9. 46–50	Ps. ***80***; 82 2 Kings ch. 5 Acts 26. 1–23	Ps. ***85***; 86 1 Macc. 3. 1–26 *or* 2 Chron. 17. 1–12 Mark 15. 1–15

October 2024

1 Tuesday — *Remigius, Bishop of Rheims, Apostle of the Franks, 533; Anthony Ashley Cooper, Earl of Shaftesbury, Social Reformer, 1885*

G	Job 3. 1–3, 11–17, 20–23 Ps. 88. 14–19 Luke 9. 51–56	Ps. 87; ***89. 1–18*** 2 Kings 6. 1–23 Acts 26. 24–end	Ps. 89. 19–end 1 Macc. 3. 27–41 *or* 2 Chron. 18. 1–27 Mark 15. 16–32

October 2024		Sunday Principal Service Weekday Eucharist	Third Service Morning Prayer	Second Service Evening Prayer
2 Wednesday				
G		Job 9. 1–12, 14–16 Ps. 88. 1–6, 11 Luke 9. 57–end	Ps. 119. 105–128 2 Kings 9. 1–16 Acts 27. 1–26	Ps. ***91***; 93 1 Macc. 3. 42–end *or* 2 Chron. 18.28 – 19.end Mark 15. 33–41
3 Thursday	*George Bell, Bishop of Chichester, Ecumenist, Peacemaker, 1958*			
G		Job 19. 21–27a Ps. 27. 13–16 Luke 10. 1–12	Ps. 90; ***92*** 2 Kings 9. 17–end Acts 27. 27–end	Ps. 94 1 Macc. 4. 1–25 *or* 2 Chron. 20. 1–23 Mark 15. 42–end
4 Friday	**Francis of Assisi, Friar, Founder of the Friars Minor, 1226**			
Gw	Com. Religious *also* Gal. 6. 14–end Luke 12. 22–34	*or* Job 38. 1, 12–21; 40. 3–5 Ps. 139. 6–11 Luke 10. 13–16	Ps. ***88***; (95) 2 Kings 12. 1–19 Acts 28. 1–16	Ps. 102 1 Macc. 4. 26–35 *or* 2 Chron. 22.10 – 23.end Mark 16. 1–8

5 Saturday

G	Job 42. 1–3, 6, 12–end Ps. 119. 169–end Luke 10. 17–24	Ps. 96; **97**; 100 2 Kings 17. 1–23 Acts 28. 17–end	Ps. 104 1 Macc. 4. 36–end *or* 2 Chron. 24. 1–22 Mark 16. 9–end **ct** *or First EP of Dedication Festival*: Ps. 24 2 Chron. 7. 11–16 John 4. 19–29 **𝔚 ct**

October 2024		Sunday Principal Service Weekday Eucharist	Third Service Morning Prayer	Second Service Evening Prayer
6 Sunday	**THE NINETEENTH SUNDAY AFTER TRINITY (Proper 22)**			
G	*Track 1* Job 1. 1; 2. 1–10 Ps. 26 Heb. 1. 1–4; 2. 5–12 Mark 10. 2–16	*Track 2* Gen. 2. 18–24 Ps. 8 Heb. 1. 1–4; 2. 5–12 Mark 10. 2–16	Ps. 123; 124 Isa. 49. 13–23 Luke 12. 1–12	Ps. 125; 126 Josh. 3. 7–end Matt. 10. 1–22
	or, if observed as Dedication Festival:			
𝔚		Gen. 28. 11–18 *or* Rev. 21. 9–14 Ps. 122 1 Pet. 2. 1–10 John 10. 22–29	*MP*: Ps. 48; 150 Hag. 2. 6–9 Heb. 10. 19–25	*EP*: Ps. 132 Jer. 7. 1–11 Luke 19. 1–10
7 Monday				
G **DEL 27**		Gal. 1. 6–12 Ps. 111. 1–6 Luke 10. 25–37	Ps. ***98***; 99; 101 2 Kings 17. 24–end Phil. 1. 1–11	Ps. ***105***† (*or* 103) 1 Macc. 6. 1–17 *or* 2 Chron. 26. 1–21 John 13. 1–11

8 Tuesday					
G			Gal. 1. 13–end Ps. 139. 1–9 Luke 10. 38–end	Ps. ***106***† (*or* 103) 2 Kings 18. 1–12 Phil. 1. 12–end	Ps. 107† 1 Macc. 6. 18–47 *or* 2 Chron. ch. 28 John 13. 12–20
9 Wednesday	*Denys, Bishop of Paris, and his Companions, Martyrs, c. 250; Robert Grosseteste, Bishop of Lincoln, Philosopher, Scientist, 1253*				
G			Gal. 2. 1–2, 7–14 Ps. 117 Luke 11. 1–4	Ps. 110; ***111***; 112 2 Kings 18. 13–end Phil. 2. 1–13	Ps. 119. 129–152 1 Macc. 7. 1–20 *or* 2 Chron. 29. 1–19 John 13. 21–30
10 Thursday	**Paulinus, Bishop of York, Missionary, 644** *Thomas Traherne, Poet, Spiritual Writer, 1674*				
Gw	Com. Missionary *esp.* Matt. 28. 16–end	*or*	Gal. 3. 1–5 *Canticle*: Benedictus Luke 11. 5–13	Ps. 113; ***115*** 2 Kings 19. 1–19 Phil. 2. 14–end	Ps. 114; ***116***; 117 1 Macc. 7. 21–end *or* 2 Chron. 29. 20–end John 13. 31–end

October 2024		Sunday Principal Service Weekday Eucharist	Third Service Morning Prayer	Second Service Evening Prayer
11 Friday	*Ethelburga, Abbess of Barking, 675; James the Deacon, Companion of Paulinus, 7th century*			
G		Gal. 3. 7–14 Ps. 111. 4–end Luke 11. 15–26	Ps. 139 2 Kings 19. 20–36 Phil. 3.1 – 4.1	Ps. ***130***; 131; 137 1 Macc. 9. 1–22 *or* 2 Chron. ch. 30 John 14. 1–14
12 Saturday	**Wilfrid of Ripon, Bishop, Missionary, 709** *Elizabeth Fry, Prison Reformer, 1845; Edith Cavell, Nurse, 1915*			
Gw	Com. Missionary *esp.* Luke 5. 1–11 *also* 1 Cor. 1. 18–25	*or* Gal. 3. 22–end Ps. 105. 1–7 Luke 11. 27–28	Ps. 120; ***121***; 122 2 Kings ch. 20 Phil. 4. 2–end	Ps. 118 1 Macc. 13. 41–end; 14. 4–15 *or* 2 Chron. 32. 1–22 John 14. 15–end **ct**
13 Sunday	**THE TWENTIETH SUNDAY AFTER TRINITY (Proper 23)**			
G	*Track 1* Job 23. 1–9, 16–end Ps. 22. 1–15 Heb. 4. 12–end Mark 10. 17–31	*Track 2* Amos 5. 6–7, 10–15 Ps. 90. 12–end Heb. 4. 12–end Mark 10. 17–31	Ps. 129; 130 Isa. 50. 4–10 Luke 13. 22–30	Ps. 127; [128] Josh. 5.13 – 6.20 Matt. 11. 20–end

14 Monday					
G **DEL 28**			Gal. 4. 21–24, 26–27, 31; 5. 1 Ps. 113 Luke 11. 29–32	Ps. 123; 124; 125; ***126*** 2 Kings 21. 1–18 1 Tim. 1. 1–17	Ps. ***127***; 128; 129 2 Macc. 4. 7–17 *or* 2 Chron. 33. 1–13 John 15. 1–11
15 Tuesday	**Teresa of Avila, Teacher, 1582**				
Gw	Com. Teacher *also* Rom. 8. 22–27	*or*	Gal. 5. 1–6 Ps. 119. 41–48 Luke 11. 37–41	Ps. ***132***; 133 2 Kings 22.1 – 23.3 1 Tim. 1.18 – 2.end	Ps. (134); ***135*** 2 Macc. 6. 12–end *or* 2 Chron. 34. 1–18 John 15. 12–17
16 Wednesday	*Nicholas Ridley, Bishop of London, and Hugh Latimer, Bishop of Worcester, Reformation Martyrs, 1555*				
G			Gal. 5. 18–end Ps. 1 Luke 11. 42–46	Ps. 119. 153–end 2 Kings 23. 4–25 1 Tim. ch. 3	Ps. 136 2 Mac. 7. 1–19 *or* 2 Chron. 34. 19–end John 15. 18–end

October 2024		Sunday Principal Service Weekday Eucharist	Third Service Morning Prayer	Second Service Evening Prayer
17 Thursday	**Ignatius, Bishop of Antioch, Martyr, c. 107**			
Gr	Com. Martyr *also* Phil. 3. 7–12 John 6. 52–58	*or* Eph. 1. 1–10 Ps. 98. 1–4 Luke 11. 47–end	Ps. ***143***; 146 2 Kings 23.36 – 24.17 1 Tim. ch. 4	Ps. ***138***; 140; 141 2 Macc. 7. 20–41 *or* 2 Chron. 35. 1–19 John 16. 1–15 *or First EP of Luke* Ps. 33 Hos. 6. 1–3 2 Tim. 3. 10–end **R ct**
18 Friday	**LUKE THE EVANGELIST**			
R		Isa. 35. 3–6 *or* Acts 16. 6–12a Ps. 147. 1–7 2 Tim. 4. 5–17 Luke 10. 1–9	*MP*: Ps. 145; 146 Isa. ch. 55 Luke 1. 1–4	*EP*: Ps. 103 Ecclus. 38. 1–14 *or* Isa. 61. 1–6 Col. 4. 7–end

19 Saturday	**Henry Martyn, Translator of the Scriptures, Missionary in India and Persia, 1812**			
Gw	Com. Missionary *esp.* Mark 16. 15–end *also* Isa. 55. 6–11	*or* Eph. 1. 15–end Ps. 8 Luke 12. 8–12	Ps. 147 2 Kings 25. 22–end 1 Tim. 5. 17–end	Ps. ***148***; 149; 150 Tobit ch. 2 *or* 2 Chron. 36. 11–end John 16. 23–end **ct**
20 Sunday	**THE TWENTY-FIRST SUNDAY AFTER TRINITY (Proper 24)**			
G	*Track 1* Job 38. 1–7 [34–end] Ps. 104. 1–10, 26, 35c (*or* 1–10) Heb. 5. 1–10 Mark 10. 35–45	*Track 2* Isa. 53. 4–end Ps. 91. 9–end Heb. 5. 1–10 Mark 10. 35–45	Ps. 133; 134; 137. 1–6 Isa. 54. 1–14 Luke 13. 31–end	Ps. 141 Josh. 14. 6–14 Matt. 12. 1–21
21 Monday				
G **DEL 29**		Eph. 2. 1–10 Ps. 100 Luke 12. 13–21	Ps. ***1***; 2; 3 Judith ch. 4 *or* Exod. 22. 21–27; 23. 1–17 1 Tim. 6. 1–10	Ps. ***4***; 7 Tobit ch. 3 *or* Mic. 1. 1–9 John 17. 1–5

October 2024		Sunday Principal Service Weekday Eucharist	Third Service Morning Prayer	Second Service Evening Prayer
22 Tuesday				
	G	Eph. 2. 12–end Ps. 85. 7–end Luke 12. 35–38	Ps. ***5***; 6; (8) Judith 5.1 – 6.4 *or* Exod. 29.38 – 30.16 1 Tim. 6. 11–end	Ps. ***9***; 10† Tobit ch. 4 *or* Mic. ch. 2 John 17. 6–19
23 Wednesday				
	G	Eph. 3. 2–12 Ps. 98 Luke 12. 39–48	Ps. 119. 1–32 Judith 6.10 – 7.7 *or* Lev. ch. 8 2 Tim. 1. 1–14	Ps. ***11***; 12; 13 Tobit 5.1 – 6.1a *or* Mic. ch. 3 John 17. 20–end
24 Thursday				
	G	Eph. 3. 14–end Ps. 33. 1–6 Luke 12. 49–53	Ps. 14; ***15***; 16 Judith 7. 19–end *or* Lev. ch. 9 2 Tim. 1.15 – 2.13	Ps. 18† Tobit 6. 1b–end *or* Mic. 4.1 – 5.1 John 18. 1–11

25 Friday	*Crispin and Crispinian, Martyrs at Rome, c. 287*				
G			Eph. 4. 1–6 Ps. 24. 1–6 Luke 12. 54–end	Ps. 17; ***19*** Judith 8. 9–end *or* Lev. 16. 2–24 2 Tim. 2. 14–end	Ps. 22 Tobit ch. 7 *or* Mic. 5. 2–end John 18. 12–27
26 Saturday	**Alfred the Great, King of the West Saxons, Scholar, 899** *Cedd, Abbot of Lastingham, Bishop of the East Saxons, 664**				
Gw	Com. Saint *also* 2 Sam. 23. 1–5 John 18. 33–37	*or*	Eph. 4. 7–16 Ps. 122 Luke 13. 1–9	Ps. 20; 21; ***23*** Judith ch. 9 *or* Lev. ch. 17 2 Tim. ch. 3	Ps. ***24***; 25 Tobit ch. 8 *or* Mic. ch. 6 John 18. 28–end **ct**

*Chad may be celebrated with Cedd on 26 October instead of 2 March.

October 2024		Sunday Principal Service Weekday Eucharist	Third Service Morning Prayer	Second Service Evening Prayer
27 Sunday	**THE LAST SUNDAY AFTER TRINITY***			
G	*Track 1* Job 42. 1–6, 10–end Ps. 34. 1–8, 19–end (*or* 1–8) Heb. 7. 23–end Mark 10. 46–end	*Track 2* Jer. 31. 7–9 Ps. 126 Heb. 7. 23–end Mark 10. 46–end	Ps. 119. 89–104 Isa. 59. 9–20 Luke 14. 1–14	Ps. 119. 121–136 Eccles. chs 11 and 12 2 Tim. 2. 1–7 *Gospel*: Luke 18. 9–14 *or First EP of Simon and Jude* Ps. 124; 125; 126 Deut. 32. 1–4 John 14. 15–26 **R ct**
	or, if being observed as Bible Sunday:			
G		Isa. 55. 1–11 Ps. 19. 7–end 2 Tim. 3.14 - 4.5 John 5. 36b–end	Ps. 119. 89–104 Isa. 45. 22–end Matt. 24. 30–35 *or* Luke 14. 1–14	Ps. 119. 1–16 2 Kings ch. 22 Col. 3. 12–17 *Gospel*: Luke 4. 14–30 *or First EP of Simon and Jude* Ps. 124; 125; 126 Deut. 32. 1–4 John 14. 15–26 **R ct**

28 Monday	**SIMON AND JUDE, APOSTLES**			
R **DEL 30**		Isa. 28. 14–16 Ps. 119. 89–96 Eph. 2. 19–end John 15. 17–end	*MP*: Ps. 116; 117 Wisd. 5. 1–16 *or* Isa. 45. 18–end Luke 6. 12–16	*EP*: Ps. 119. 1–16 1 Macc. 2. 42–66 *or* Jer. 3. 11–18 Jude 1–4, 17–end
29 Tuesday	**James Hannington, Bishop of Eastern Equatorial Africa, Martyr in Uganda, 1885**			
Gr	Com. Martyr *esp.* Matt. 10. 28–39 *or*	Eph. 5. 21–end Ps. 128 Luke 13. 18–21	Ps. 32; ***36*** Judith ch. 11 *or* Lev. 23. 1–22 2 Tim. 4. 9–end	Ps. 33 Tobit ch. 10 *or* Mic. 7. 8–end John 19. 17–30
30 Wednesday				
G		Eph. 6. 1–9 Ps. 145. 10–20 Luke 13. 22–30	Ps. 34 Judith ch. 12 *or* Lev. 23. 23–end Titus ch. 1	Ps. 119. 33–56 Tobit ch. 11 *or* Hab. 1. 1–11 John 19. 31–end

*If the Dedication Festival is kept on this Sunday, use the provision given on 5 and 6 October.

October/ November 2024		Sunday Principal Service Weekday Eucharist	Third Service Morning Prayer	Second Service Evening Prayer
31 Thursday	*Martin Luther, Reformer, 1546*			
G		Eph. 6. 10–20 Ps. 144. 1–2, 9–11 Luke 13. 31–end	Ps. 37† Judith ch. 13 *or* Lev. 24. 1–9 Titus ch. 2	*First EP of All Saints* Ps. 1; 5 Ecclus. 44. 1–15 *or* Isa. 40. 27–end Rev. 19. 6–10 **𝔚 ct** *or, if All Saints is observed on 3 November*: Tobit ch. 12 *or* Hab. 1.12 – 2.5 John 20. 1–10

November 2024

1 Friday	**ALL SAINTS' DAY**			
𝔚		Wisd. 3. 1–9 *or* Isa. 25. 6–9 Ps. 24. 1–6 Rev. 21. 1–6a John 11. 32–44	*MP*: Ps. 15; 84; 149 Isa. ch. 35 Luke 9. 18–27	*EP*: Ps. 148; 150 Isa. 65. 17–end Heb. 11.32 – 12.2

or, if the readings above are used on Sunday 3 November:

𝔚			Isa. 56. 3–8 *or* 2 Esdras 2. 42–end Ps. 33. 1–5 Heb. 12. 18–24 Matt. 5. 1–12	*MP*: 111; 112; 117 Wisd. 5. 1–16 *or* Jer. 31. 31–34 2 Cor. 4. 5–12	*EP*: Ps. 145 Isa. 66. 20–23 Col. 1. 9–14

or, if kept as a feria:

G			Phil. 1. 1–11 Ps. 111 Luke 14. 1–6	Ps. 31 Judith 15. 1–13 *or* Lev. 25. 1–24 Titus ch. 3	Ps. 35 Tobit 13.1 – 14.1 *or* Hab. 2. 6–end John 20. 11–18

2 Saturday **Commemoration of the Faithful Departed (All Souls' Day)**

Rp *or* **Gp**	Lam. 3. 17–26, 31–33 *or* Wisd. 3. 1–9 Ps. 23 *or* Ps. 27. 1–6, 16–end Rom. 5. 5–11 *or* 1 Pet. 1. 3–9 John 5. 19–25 *or* John 6. 37–40	*or*	Phil. 1. 18–26 Ps. 42. 1–7 Luke 14. 1, 7–11	Ps. 41; ***42***; 43 Judith 15.14 – 16.end *or* Num. 6. 1–5, 21–end Philem.	Ps. 45; ***46*** Tobit 14. 2–end *or* Hab. 3. 2–19a John 20. 19–end **ct**

November 2024		Sunday Principal Service Weekday Eucharist	Third Service Morning Prayer	Second Service Evening Prayer
3 Sunday	**THE FOURTH SUNDAY BEFORE ADVENT**			
R *or* **G**		Deut. 6. 1–9 Ps. 119. 1–8 Heb. 9. 11–14 Mark 12. 28–34	Ps. 112; 149 Jer. 31. 31–34 1 John 3. 1–3	Ps. 145 (*or* 145. 1–9) Dan. 2. 1–48 (*or* 2. 1–11, 25–48) Rev. 7. 9–end *Gospel*: Matt. 5. 1–12
	or ALL SAINTS' SUNDAY (see readings for 1 November throughout the day)			
𝔚				
4 Monday				
R *or* **G** **DEL 31**		Phil. 2. 1–4 Ps. 131 Luke 14. 12–14	Ps. ***2***; 146 *alt*. Ps. 44 Dan. ch. 1 Rev. ch. 1	Ps. ***92***; 96; 97 *alt*. Ps. ***47***; 49 Isa. 1. 1–20 Matt. 1. 18–end
5 Tuesday				
R *or* **G**		Phil. 2. 5–11 Ps. 22. 22–27 Luke 14. 15–24	Ps. ***5***; 147. 1–12 *alt*. Ps. ***48***; 52 Dan. 2. 1–24 Rev. 2. 1–11	Ps. 98; 99; ***100*** *alt*. Ps. 50 Isa. 1. 21–end Matt. 2. 1–15

6 Wednesday	*Leonard, Hermit, 6th century; William Temple, Archbishop of Canterbury, Teacher, 1944*				
R *or* **G**			Phil. 2. 12–18 Ps. 27. 1–5 Luke 14. 25–33	Ps. ***9***; 147. 13–end *alt.* Ps. 119. 57–80 Dan. 2. 25–end Rev. 2. 12–end	Ps. 111; ***112***; 116 *alt.* Ps. ***59***; 60; (67) Isa. 2. 1–11 Matt. 2. 16–end
7 Thursday	**Willibrord of York, Bishop, Apostle of Frisia, 739**				
Rw *or* **Gw**	Com. Missionary *esp.* Isa. 52. 7–10 Matt. 28. 16–end	*or*	Phil. 3. 3–8a Ps. 105. 1–7 Luke 15. 1–10	Ps. 11; ***15***; 148 *alt.* Ps. 56; ***57***; (63†) Dan. 3. 1–18 Rev. 3. 1–13	Ps. 118 *alt.* Ps. 61; ***62***; 64 Isa. 2. 12–end Matt. ch. 3
8 Friday	**The Saints and Martyrs of England**				
Rw *or* **Gw**	Isa. 61. 4–9 *or* Ecclus. 44. 1–15 Ps. 15 Rev. 19. 5–10 John 17. 18–23	*or*	Phil. 3.17 - 4.1 Ps. 122 Luke 16. 1–8	Ps. ***16***; 149 *alt.* Ps. ***51***; 54 Dan. 3. 19–end Rev. 3. 14–end	Ps. 137; 138; ***143*** *alt.* Ps. 38 Isa. 3. 1–15 Matt. 4. 1–11

November 2024		Sunday Principal Service Weekday Eucharist	Third Service Morning Prayer	Second Service Evening Prayer
9 Saturday	*Margery Kempe, Mystic, c. 1440*			
R *or* **G**		Phil. 4. 10–19 Ps. 112 Luke 16. 9–15	Ps. ***18. 31–end***; 150 *alt.* Ps. 68 Dan. 4. 1–18 Rev. ch. 4	Ps. 145 *alt.* Ps. 65; ***66*** Isa. 4.2 – 5.7 Matt. 4. 12–22 **ct**
10 Sunday	**THE THIRD SUNDAY BEFORE ADVENT** (Remembrance Sunday)			
R *or* **G**		Jonah 3. 1–5, 10 Ps. 62. 5–end Heb. 9. 24–end Mark 1. 14–20	Ps. 136 Mic. 4. 1–5 Phil. 4. 6–9	Ps. 46; [82] Isa. 10.33 – 11.9 John 14. 1–29 (*or* 23–29)
11 Monday	**Martin, Bishop of Tours, c. 397**			
Rw *or* **Gw** **DEL 32**	Com. Bishop *also* 1 Thess. 5. 1–11 Matt. 25. 34–40 *or*	Titus 1. 1–9 Ps. 24. 1–6 Luke 17. 1–6	Ps. 19; ***20*** *alt.* Ps. 71 Dan. 4. 19–end Rev. ch. 5	Ps. 34 *alt.* Ps. ***72***; 75 Isa. 5. 8–24 Matt. 4.23 – 5.12

12 Tuesday					
R *or* **G**			Titus 2. 1–8, 11–14 Ps. 37. 3–5, 30–32 Luke 17. 7–10	Ps. ***21***; 24 *alt*. Ps. 73 Dan. 5. 1–12 Rev. ch. 6	Ps. 36; ***40*** *alt*. Ps. 74 Isa. 5. 25–end Matt. 5. 13–20
13 Wednesday	**Charles Simeon, Priest, Evangelical Divine, 1836**				
Rw *or* **Gw**	Com. Pastor *esp*. Mal. 2. 5–7 *also* Col. 1. 3–8 Luke 8. 4–8	*or*	Titus 3. 1–7 Ps. 23 Luke 17. 11–19	Ps. ***23***; 25 *alt*. Ps. 77 Dan. 5. 13–end Rev. 7. 1–4, 9–end	Ps. 37 *alt*. Ps. 119. 81–104 Isa. ch. 6 Matt. 5. 21–37
14 Thursday	*Samuel Seabury, first Anglican Bishop in North America, 1796*				
R *or* **G**			Philem. 7–20 Ps. 146. 4–end Luke 17. 20–25	Ps. ***26***; 27 *alt*. Ps. 78. 1–39† Dan. ch. 6 Rev. ch. 8	Ps. 42; ***43*** *alt*. Ps. 78. 40–end† Isa. 7. 1–17 Matt. 5. 38–end
15 Friday					
R *or* **G**			2 John 4–9 Ps. 119. 1–8 Luke 17. 26–end	Ps. 28; ***32*** *alt*. Ps. 55 Dan. 7. 1–14 Rev. 9. 1–12	Ps. 31 *alt*. Ps. 69 Isa. 8. 1–15 Matt. 6. 1–18

November 2024		Sunday Principal Service Weekday Eucharist	Third Service Morning Prayer	Second Service Evening Prayer
16 Saturday	**Margaret, Queen of Scotland, Philanthropist, Reformer of the Church, 1093** *Edmund Rich of Abingdon, Archbishop of Canterbury, 1240*			
Rw *or* **Gw**	Com. Saint *also* Prov. 31. 10–12, 20, 26–end 1 Cor. 12.13 – 13.3 Matt. 25. 34–end	*or* 3 John 5–8 Ps. 112 Luke 18. 1–8	Ps. 33 *alt.* Ps. ***76***; 79 Dan. 7. 15–end Rev. 9. 13–end	Ps. 84; ***86*** *alt.* Ps. 81; ***84*** Isa. 8.16 – 9.7 Matt. 6. 19–end **ct**
17 Sunday	**THE SECOND SUNDAY BEFORE ADVENT**			
R *or* **G**		Dan. 12. 1–3 Ps. 16 Heb. 10. 11–14 [15–18] 19–25 Mark 13. 1–8	Ps. 96 1 Sam. 9.27 – 10.2a; 10. 17–26 Matt. 13. 31–35	Ps. 95 Dan. ch. 3. (*or* 3. 13–end) Matt. 13. 24–30, 36–43
18 Monday	**Elizabeth of Hungary, Princess of Thuringia, Philanthropist, 1231**			
Rw *or* **Gw** **DEL 33**	Com. Saint *esp.* Matt. 25. 31–end *also* Prov. 31. 10–end	*or* Rev. 1. 1–4; 2. 1–5 Ps. 1 Luke 18. 35–end	Ps. 46; ***47*** *alt.* Ps. ***80***; 82 Dan. 8. 1–14 Rev. ch. 10	Ps. 70; ***71*** *alt.* Ps. ***85***; 86 Isa. 9.8 – 10.4 Matt. 7. 1–12

19 Tuesday	**Hilda, Abbess of Whitby, 680** *Mechtild, Béguine of Magdeburg, Mystic, 1280*				
Rw *or* **Gw**	Com. Religious *esp.* Isa. 61.10 – 62.5	*or*	Rev. 3. 1–6, 14–end Ps. 15 Luke 19. 1–10	Ps. 48; ***52*** *alt.* Ps. 87; ***89. 1–18*** Dan. 8. 15–end Rev. 11. 1–14	Ps. ***67***; 72 *alt.* Ps. 89. 19–end Isa. 10. 5–19 Matt. 7. 13–end
20 Wednesday	**Edmund, King of the East Angles, Martyr, 870** *Priscilla Lydia Sellon, a Restorer of the Religious Life in the Church of England, 1876*				
R *or* **Gr**	Com. Martyr *also* Prov. 20. 28; 21. 1–4, 7	*or*	Rev. ch. 4 Ps. 150 Luke 19. 11–28	Ps. ***56***; 57 *alt.* Ps. 119. 105–128 Dan. 9. 1–19 Rev. 11. 15–end	Ps. 73 *alt.* Ps. ***91***; 93 Isa. 10. 20–32 Matt. 8. 1–13
21 Thursday					
R *or* **G**			Rev. 5. 1–10 Ps. 149. 1–5 Luke 19. 41–44	Ps. 61; ***62*** *alt.* Ps. 90; ***92*** Dan. 9. 20–end Rev. ch. 12	Ps. 74; ***76*** *alt.* Ps. 94 Isa. 10.33 – 11.9 Matt. 8. 14–22

November 2023		Sunday Principal Service Weekday Eucharist	Third Service Morning Prayer	Second Service Evening Prayer
22 Friday	*Cecilia, Martyr at Rome, c. 230*			
R *or* **G**		Rev. 10. 8–end Ps. 119. 65–72 Luke 19. 45–end	Ps. ***63***; 65 *alt.* Ps. ***88***; (95) Dan. 10.1 – 11.1 Rev. 13. 1–10	Ps. 77 *alt.* Ps. 102 Isa. 11.10 – 12.end Matt. 8. 23–end
23 Saturday	**Clement, Bishop of Rome, Martyr, c. 100**			
R *or* **Gr**	Com. Martyr *also* Phil. 3.17 – 4.3 Matt. 16. 13–19 *or*	Rev. 11. 4–12 Ps. 144. 1–9 Luke 20. 27–40	Ps. 78. 1–39 *alt.* Ps. 96; ***97***; 100 Dan. ch. 12 Rev. 13. 11–end	Ps. 78. 40–end *alt.* Ps. 104 Isa. 13. 1–13 Matt. 9. 1–17 **ct** *or First EP of Christ the King* Ps. 99; 100 Isa. 10.33 – 11.9 1 Tim. 6. 11–16 **R** *or* **W ct**

24 Sunday	**CHRIST THE KING** The Sunday Next Before Advent			
R *or* **W**		Dan. 7. 9–10, 13–14 Ps. 93 Rev. 1. 4b–8 John 18. 33–37	*MP*: Ps. 29; 110 Isa. 32. 1–8 Rev. 3. 7–end	*EP*: Ps. 72 (*or* 72. 1–7) Dan. ch. 5 John 6. 1–15
25 Monday	*Catherine of Alexandria, Martyr, 4th century; Isaac Watts, Hymn Writer, 1748*			
R *or* **G** **DEL 34**		Rev. 14. 1–5 Ps. 24. 1–6 Luke 21. 1–4	Ps. 92; ***96*** *alt*. Ps. **98**; 99; 101 Isa. 40. 1–11 Rev. 14. 1–13	Ps. ***80***; 81 *alt*. Ps. 105† (*or* 103) Isa. 14. 3–20 Matt. 9. 18–34
26 Tuesday				
R *or* **G**		Rev. 14. 14–19 Ps. 96 Luke 21. 5–11	Ps. ***97***; 98; 100 *alt*. Ps. ***106***† (*or* 103) Isa. 40. 12–26 Rev. 14.14 – 15.end	Ps. 99; ***101*** *alt*. Ps. 107† Isa. ch. 17 Matt. 9.35 – 10.15

November/ December 2024		Sunday Principal Service Weekday Eucharist	Third Service Morning Prayer	Second Service Evening Prayer
27 Wednesday				
R *or* **G**		Rev. 15. 1–4 Ps. 98 Luke 21. 12–19	Ps. 110; 111; ***112*** *alt*. Ps. 110; ***111***; 112 Isa. 40.27 – 41.7 Rev. 16. 1–11	Ps. 121; ***122***; 123; 124 *alt*. Ps. 119. 129–152 Isa. ch. 19 Matt. 10. 16–33
28 Thursday				
R *or* **G**		Rev. 18. 1–2, 21–23; 19. 1–3, 9 Ps. 100 Luke 21. 20–28	Ps. ***125***; 126; 127; 128 *alt*. Ps. 113; ***115*** Isa. 41. 8–20 Rev. 16. 12–end	Ps. 131; 132; ***133*** *alt*. Ps. 114; ***116***; 117 Isa. 21. 1–12 Matt. 10.34 – 11.1
29 Friday				
R *or* **G**		Rev. 20.1–4, 11 – 21.2 Ps. 84. 1–6 Luke 21. 29–33	Ps. 139 *alt*. Ps. 139 Isa. 41.21 – 42.9 Rev. ch. 17	Ps. ***146***; 147 *alt*. Ps. ***130***; 131; 137 Isa. 22. 1–14 Matt. 11. 2–19 *or First EP of Andrew the Apostle* Ps. 48 Isa. 49. 1–9a 1 Cor. 4. 9–16 **R ct**

Day of Intercession and Thanksgiving for the Missionary Work of the Church

Isa. 49. 1–6; Isa. 52. 7–10; Mic. 4. 1–5
Ps. 2; 46; 47
Acts 17. 12–end; 2 Cor. 5.14 – 6.2; Eph. 2. 13–end
Matt. 5. 13–16; Matt. 28. 16–end; John 17. 20–end

30 Saturday **ANDREW THE APOSTLE**

R	Isa. 52. 7–10 Ps. 19. 1–6 Rom. 10. 12–18 Matt. 4. 18–22	*MP*: Ps. 47; 147. 1–12 Ezek. 47. 1–12 *or* Ecclus. 14. 20–end John 12. 20–32	*EP*: Ps. 87; 96 Zech. 8. 20–end John 1. 35–42

December 2024

1 Sunday **THE FIRST SUNDAY OF ADVENT**
Common Worship Year C begins

P	Jer. 33. 14–16 Ps. 25. 1–9 1 Thess. 3. 9–end Luke 21. 25–36	Ps. 44 Isa. 51. 4–11 Rom. 13. 11–end	Ps. 9 (*or* 9. 1–8) Joel 3. 9–end Rev. 14.13 – 15.4 *Gospel*: John 3. 1–17

December 2024		Sunday Principal Service Weekday Eucharist	Third Service Morning Prayer	Second Service Evening Prayer
2 Monday	Daily Eucharistic Lectionary Year 1 begins			
P		Isa. 2. 1–5 Ps. 122 Matt. 8. 5–11	Ps. ***50***; 54 *alt*. Ps. ***1***; 2; 3 Isa. 42. 18–end Rev. ch. 19	Ps. 70; ***71*** *alt*. Ps. ***4***; 7 Isa. 25. 1–9 Matt. 12. 1–21
3 Tuesday	*Francis Xavier, Missionary, Apostle of the Indies, 1552*			
P		Isa. 11. 1–10 Ps. 72. 1–4, 18–19 Luke 10. 21–24	Ps. ***80***; 82 *alt*. Ps. ***5***; 6; (8) Isa. 43. 1–13 Rev. ch. 20	Ps. ***74***; 75 *alt*. Ps. ***9***; 10† Isa. 26. 1–13 Matt. 12. 22–37
4 Wednesday	*John of Damascus, Monk, Teacher, c. 749; Nicholas Ferrar, Deacon, Founder of the Little Gidding Community, 1637*			
P		Isa. 25. 6–10a Ps. 23 Matt. 15. 29–37	Ps. 5; ***7*** *alt*. Ps. 119. 1–32 Isa. 43. 14–end Rev. 21. 1–8	Ps. 76; ***77*** *alt*. Ps. ***11***; 12; 13 Isa. 28. 1–13 Matt. 12. 38–end

5 Thursday					
P			Isa. 26. 1–6 Ps. 118. 18–27a Matt. 7. 21, 24–27	Ps. ***42***; 43 *alt*. Ps. 14; ***15***; 16 Isa. 44. 1–8 Rev. 21. 9–21	Ps. ***40***; 46 *alt*. Ps. 18† Isa. 28. 14–end Matt. 13. 1–23
6 Friday	**Nicholas, Bishop of Myra, *c*. 326**				
Pw	Com. Bishop *also* Isa. 61. 1–3 1 Tim. 6. 6–11 Mark 10. 13–16	*or*	Isa. 29. 17–end Ps. 27. 1–4, 16–17 Matt. 9. 27–31	Ps. ***25***; 26 *alt*. Ps. 17; ***19*** Isa. 44. 9–23 Rev. 21.22 – 22.5	Ps. 16; ***17*** *alt*. Ps. 22 Isa. 29. 1–14 Matt. 13. 24–43
7 Saturday	**Ambrose, Bishop of Milan, Teacher, 397**				
Pw	Com. Teacher *also* Isa. 41. 9b–13 Luke 22. 24–30	*or*	Isa. 30. 19–21, 23–26 Ps. 146. 4–9 Matt. 9.35 – 10.1, 6–8	Ps. ***9***; 10 *alt*. Ps. 20; 21; ***23*** Isa. 44.24 – 45.13 Rev. 22. 6–end	Ps. ***27***; 28 *alt*. Ps. ***24***; 25 Isa. 29. 15–end Matt. 13. 44–end **ct**

December 2024		Sunday Principal Service Weekday Eucharist	Third Service Morning Prayer	Second Service Evening Prayer
8 Sunday	**THE SECOND SUNDAY OF ADVENT**			
P		Baruch ch. 5 *or* Mal. 3. 1–4 *Canticle*: Benedictus Phil. 1. 3–11 Luke 3. 1–6	Ps. 80 Isa. 64. 1–7 Matt. 11. 2–11	Ps. 75; [76] Isa. 40. 1–11 Luke 1. 1–25
9 Monday				
P		Isa. ch. 35 Ps. 85. 7–end Luke 5. 17–26	Ps. 44 *alt.* Ps. 27; ***30*** Isa. 45. 14–end 1 Thess. ch. 1	Ps. ***144***; 146 *alt.* Ps. 26; ***28***; 29 Isa. 30. 1–18 Matt. 14. 1–12
10 Tuesday				
P		Isa. 40. 1–11 Ps. 96. 1, 10–end Matt. 18. 12–14	Ps. ***56***; 57 *alt.* Ps. 32; ***36*** Isa. ch. 46 1 Thess. 2. 1–12	Ps. ***11***; 12; 13 *alt.* Ps. 33 Isa. 30. 19–end Matt. 14. 13–end

11 Wednesday	Ember Day			
P		Isa. 40. 25–end Ps. 103. 8–13 Matt. 11. 28–end	Ps. ***62***; 63 *alt.* Ps. 34 Isa. ch. 47 1 Thess. 2. 13–end	Ps. ***10***; 14 *alt.* Ps. 119. 33–56 Isa. ch. 31 Matt. 15. 1–20
12 Thursday				
P		Isa. 41. 13–20 Ps. 145. 1, 8–13 Matt. 11. 11–15	Ps. 53; ***54***; 60 *alt.* Ps. 37† Isa. 48. 1–11 1 Thess. ch. 3	Ps. 73 *alt.* Ps. 39; ***40*** Isa. ch. 32 Matt. 15. 21–28
13 Friday	**Lucy, Martyr at Syracuse, 304** Ember Day *Samuel Johnson, Moralist, 1784*			
Pr	Com. Martyr *also* Wisd. 3. 1–7 2 Cor. 4. 6–15	*or* Isa. 48. 17–19 Ps. 1 Matt. 11. 16–19	Ps. 85; ***86*** *alt.* Ps. 31 Isa. 48. 12–end 1 Thess. 4. 1–12	Ps. 82; ***90*** *alt.* Ps. 35 Isa. 33. 1–22 Matt. 15. 29–end

December 2024		Sunday Principal Service Weekday Eucharist	Third Service Morning Prayer	Second Service Evening Prayer
14 Saturday	**John of the Cross, Poet, Teacher, 1591** Ember Day			
Pw	Com. Teacher *or* *esp.* 1 Cor. 2. 1–10 *also* John 14. 18–23	Ecclus. 48. 1–4, 9–11 *or* 2 Kings 2. 9–12 Ps. 80. 1–4, 18–19 Matt. 17. 10–13	Ps. 145 *alt.* Ps. 41; ***42***; 43 Isa. 49. 1–13 1 Thess. 4. 13–end	Ps. 93; ***94*** *alt.* Ps. 45; ***46*** Isa. ch. 35 Matt. 16. 1–12 **ct**
15 Sunday	**THE THIRD SUNDAY OF ADVENT**			
P		Zeph. 3. 14–end *Canticle*: Isa. 12. 2–end *or* Ps. 146. 4–end Phil. 4. 4–7 Luke 3. 7–18	Ps. 12; 14 Isa. 25. 1–9 1 Cor. 4. 1–5	Ps. 50. 1–6; [62] Isa. ch. 35 Luke 1. 57–66 [67–end]
16 Monday				
P		Num. 24. 2–7, 15–17 Ps. 25. 3–8 Matt. 21. 23–27	Ps. 40 *alt.* Ps. 44 Isa. 49. 14–25 1 Thess. 5. 1–11	Ps. 25; ***26*** *alt.* Ps. ***47***; 49 Isa. 38. 1–8, 21–22 Matt. 16. 13–end

17 Tuesday	O Sapientia *Eglantyne Jebb, Social Reformer, Founder of 'Save the Children', 1928*		
P	Gen. 49. 2, 8–10 Ps. 72. 1-5, 18–19 Matt. 1. 1-17	Ps. ***70***; 74 *alt*. Ps. ***48***; 52 Isa. ch. 50 1 Thess. 5. 12–end	Ps. ***50***; 54 *alt*. Ps. 50 Isa. 38. 9–20 Matt. 17. 1–13
18 Wednesday			
P	Jer. 23. 5–8 Ps. 72. 1–2, 12–13, 18–end Matt. 1. 18–24	Ps. ***75***; 96 *alt*. Ps. 119. 57–80 Isa. 51. 1–8 2 Thess. ch. 1	Ps. 25; ***82*** *alt*. Ps. ***59***; 60; (67) Isa. ch. 39 Matt. 17. 14–21
19 Thursday			
P	Judg. 13. 2–7, 24–end Ps. 71. 3–8 Luke 1. 5–25	Ps. 144; ***146*** Isa. 51. 9–16 2 Thess. ch. 2	Ps. 10; ***57*** Zeph. 1.1 – 2.3 Matt. 17. 22–end
20 Friday			
P	Isa. 7. 10–14 Ps. 24. 1–6 Luke 1. 26–38	Ps. ***46***; 95 Isa. 51. 17–end 2 Thess. ch. 3	Ps. ***4***; 9 Zeph. 3. 1–13 Matt. 18. 1–20

December 2024		Sunday Principal Service Weekday Eucharist	Third Service Morning Prayer	Second Service Evening Prayer
21 Saturday*				
P		Zeph. 3. 14–18 Ps. 33. 1–4, 11–12, 20–end Luke 1. 39–45	Ps. ***121***; 122; 123 Isa. 52. 1–12 Jude	Ps. 80; ***84*** Zeph. 3. 14–end Matt. 18. 21–end **ct**
22 Sunday	**THE FOURTH SUNDAY OF ADVENT**			
P		Mic. 5. 2–5a *Canticle*: Magnificat *or* Ps. 80. 1–8 Heb. 10. 5–10 Luke 1. 39–45 [46–55]	Ps. 144 Isa. 32. 1–8 Rev. 22. 6–end	Ps. 123; [131] Isa. 10.33 – 11.10 Matt. 1. 18–end
23 Monday				
P		Mal. 3. 1–4; 4. 5–end Ps. 25. 3–9 Luke 1. 57–66	Ps. 128; 129; ***130***; 131 Isa. 52.13 – 53.end 2 Pet. 1. 1–15	Ps. 89. 1–37 Mal. 1. 1, 6–end Matt. 19. 1–12

24 Tuesday	**CHRISTMAS EVE**			
P		*Morning Eucharist* 2 Sam. 7. 1–5, 8–11, 16 Ps. 89. 2, 19–27 Acts 13. 16–26 Luke 1. 67–79	Ps. ***45***; 113 Isa. ch. 54 2 Pet. 1.16 – 2.3	Ps. 85 Zech. ch. 2 Rev. 1. 1–8
25 Wednesday	**CHRISTMAS DAY**			
𝔚	*Any of the following sets of readings may be used on the evening of Christmas Eve and on Christmas Day. Set III should be used at some service during the celebration.*	*I* Isa. 9. 2–7 Ps. 96 Titus 2. 11–14 Luke 2. 1–14 [15–20] *II* Isa. 62. 6–end Ps. 97 Titus 3. 4–7 Luke 2. [1–7] 8–20 *III* Isa. 52. 7–10 Ps. 98 Heb. 1. 1–4 [5–12] John 1. 1–14	*MP*: Ps. ***110***; 117 Isa. 62. 1–5 Matt. 1. 18–end	*EP*: Ps. 8 Isa. 65. 17–25 Phil. 2. 5–11 *or* Luke 2. 1–20 *if it has not been used at the principal service of the day*

*Thomas the Apostle may be celebrated on 21 December instead of 3 July.

December 2024		Sunday Principal Service Weekday Eucharist	Third Service Morning Prayer	Second Service Evening Prayer
26 Thursday	**STEPHEN, DEACON, FIRST MARTYR**			
R		2 Chron. 24. 20–22 *or* Acts 7. 51–end Ps. 119. 161–168 Acts 7. 51–end *or* Gal. 2. 16b–20 Matt. 10. 17–22	*MP*: Ps. ***13***; 31. 1–8; 150 Jer. 26. 12–15 Acts ch. 6	*EP*: Ps. 57; ***86*** Gen. 4. 1–10 Matt. 23. 34–end
27 Friday	**JOHN, APOSTLE AND EVANGELIST**			
W		Exod. 33. 7–11a Ps. 117 1 John ch. 1 John 21. 19b–end	*MP*: Ps. **21**; 147. 13–end Exod. 33. 12–end 1 John 2. 1–11	*EP*: Ps. 97 Isa. 6. 1–8 1 John 5. 1–12
28 Saturday	**THE HOLY INNOCENTS**			
R		Jer. 31. 15–17 Ps. 124 1 Cor. 1. 26–29 Matt. 2. 13–18	*MP*: Ps. **36**; 146 Baruch 4. 21–27 *or* Gen. 37. 13–20 Matt. 18. 1–10	*EP*: Ps. 123; ***128*** Isa. 49. 14–25 Mark 10. 13–16

29 Sunday	THE FIRST SUNDAY OF CHRISTMAS			
W		1 Sam. 2. 18–20, 26 Ps. 148 (*or* 148. 1–6) Col. 3. 12–17 Luke 2. 41–end	Ps. 105. 1–11 Isa. 41.21 – 42.1 1 John 1. 1–7	Ps. 132 Isa. ch. 61 Gal. 3.27 – 4.7 *Gospel*: Luke 2. 15–21
30 Monday				
W		1 John 2. 12–17 Ps. 96. 7–10 Luke 2. 36–40	Ps. 111; 112; ***113*** Isa. 59. 1–15a John 1. 19–28	Ps. ***65***; 84 Jonah ch. 2 Col. 1. 15–23
31 Tuesday	*John Wyclif, Reformer, 1384*			
W		1 John 2. 18–21 Ps. 96. 1, 11–end John 1. 1–18	Ps. 102 Isa. 59. 15b–end John 1. 29–34	Ps. ***90***; 148 Jonah chs 3 & 4 Col. 1.24 – 2.7 *or First EP of The Naming of Jesus* Ps. 148 Jer. 23. 1–6 Col. 2. 8–15 **ct**

THE CHURCH OF ENGLAND

Province of Canterbury

Canterbury www.canterburydiocese.org

Archbishop - The Most Revd and Rt Hon. J. P. Welby, BA, MA, Primate of All England and Metropolitan [*Lambeth Palace, London, SE1 7JU* and *Old Palace, Canterbury, CT1 2EE*] [Justin Cantuar]

Suffragan Bishop - *Dover*, R. J. Hudson-Wilkin, MBE, BPhil

Dean - D. R. M. Monteith, BSc, BTh, MA, Hon. LLD

Archdeacons - *Canterbury*, W. J. Adam, BA, LLM, PhD; *Ashford*, D. N. Miller, BSocSc, BTh; *Maidstone*, A. Sewell, BSc

Diocesan Secretary - S. R. Taylor, MBE, MA (*Acting*), Diocesan House, Lady Wootton's Green, Canterbury, CT1 1NQ. Tel: 01227 459382 email: staylor@diocant.org

London www.london.anglican.org

Bishop - S. E. Mullally, DBE, BSc, MSc, Hon DSc [*The Old Deanery, Dean's Court, London, EC4V 5AA*] [Sarah Londin]

Area Bishops - *Kensington*, E. G. Ineson, BA, MPhil, PhD; *Willesden*, L. Nsenga-Ngoy, BA, MA; *Edmonton*, R. J. Wickham, BA, MA; *Stepney*, J. W. Grenfell, BA, MA, DPhil

Suffragan Bishops - *Fulham*, J. M. R. Baker, BA, MPhil; *Islington*, R. C. Thorpe, BSc, BTh

Dean - A. Tremlett, BA, MA, MPhil

Archdeacons - *London*, L. J. Miller, BA, MA; *Hackney*, P. J. Farley-Moore, BA, MA; *Hampstead*, J. E. I. Hawkins, BD; *Charing Cross*, A. Atkinson, BA; *Middlesex*, R. S. Frank; *Northolt*, C. R. Pickford, BA, MA

General Secretary - R. Gough, London Diocesan House, 36 Causton Street, London, SW1P 4AU. Tel: 020 7932 1100 email: richard.gough@london.anglican.org

Collegiate Church of St Peter, Westminster

Dean - D. M. Hoyle, MBE, BA, MA, PhD, Hon. DLitt

Winchester www.winchester.anglican.org

Bishop - D. M. Sellin, MA (*Acting*) [*Wolvesey, Winchester, SO23 9ND*]

Suffragan Bishops - *Southampton*, D. M. Sellin, MA; *Basingstoke*, D. G. Williams, BSocSc

Dean - C. Ogle, BA, MA, MPhil

Archdeacons - *Bournemouth* (*Vacant*); *Winchester*, R. H. G. Brand, BA, MA

Diocesan Chief Executive (*Vacant*), Diocesan Office, Old Alresford Place, Alresford, SO24 9DH. Tel: 01962 737305

Bath and Wells www.bathandwells.org.uk

Bishop - N. M. R. Beasley, BSc, DPhil, BA [*The Bishop's Palace, Wells, BA5 2PD*] [Michael Bath and Wells]

Suffragan Bishop - *Taunton*, R. E. Worsley, BA, MA, LTh

Dean - J. H. Davies, DL, BA, MA, MPhil, PhD

Archdeacons - *Wells*, A. E. Gell, BA, MA, MBBS; *Bath*, A. Youings, BSc, PhD; *Taunton*, S. J. Hill, BA, PGCE, MA

Chief Executive (*Vacant*), Diocesan Office, Flourish House, Cathedral Park, Wells, BA5 1FD. Tel: 01749 670777

Birmingham https://cofebirmingham.com

Bishop (*Vacant*) [*Bishop's Croft, Old Church Road, Harborne, Birmingham, B17 0BG*]

Suffragan Bishop - *Aston*, A. E. Hollinghurst, BA, MSt

Dean - M. Thompson, BA, MA, MPhil

Archdeacons - *Aston*, S. D. Heathfield, BMus, BTh; *Birmingham*, J. C. Tomlinson, BA, MA

Diocesan Secretary - J. Smart, Diocesan Office, 1 Colmore Row, Birmingham, B3 2BJ. Tel: 0121 426 0400

Bristol www.bristol.anglican.org

Bishop - V. F. Faull, BA, MA [*The Bishop of Bristol's Office, Church Lane, Winterbourne, Bristol, BS36 1SG*] [Vivienne Bristol]

Suffragan Bishop - *Swindon*, L. S. Rayfield, BSc, PhD, SOSc

Dean - A. K. Ford, BA, MA, BTh, MA, PhD

Archdeacons - *Bristol*, N. M. Warwick, BA, MBA; *Malmesbury*, C. P. Bryan, BA

Diocesan Secretary - R. Leaman, Diocesan Office, First Floor, Hillside House, 1500 Parkway North, Stoke Gifford, Bristol, BS34 8YU. Tel: 0117 906 0100 email: richard.leaman@bristoldiocese.org

Chelmsford www.chelmsford.anglican.org

Bishop - G. E. Francis-Dehqani, BA, MA, PhD [*Bishopscourt, Main Road, Margaretting, Ingatestone, CM4 0HD*] [Guli Chelmsford]

Area Bishops - *Barking*, L. Cullens, BA; *Bradwell* (*Vacant*); *Colchester*, R. A. B. Morris, BSc, BA, MA, ARCS

Dean - N. J. Henshall, BA, MA

Archdeacons - *Barking*, C. M. Burke, LLB, MA; *Chelmsford* (*Vacant*); *Colchester*, R. J. Patten, BA, MMus; *Southend*, M. A. Power; *Stansted*, R. L. C. King, MA; *West Ham*, E. W. Cockett, BA; *Harlow*, V. A. Herrick, BA, MA, LTCL

Chief Executive - M. Southworth, Diocesan Office, 53 New Street, Chelmsford, CM1 1AT. Tel: 01245 294909 email: msouthworth@chelmsford.anglican.org

Chichester www.chichester.anglican.org

Bishop - M. C. Warner, BA, MA, PhD [*The Palace, Chichester, PO19 1PY*] [Martin Cicestr]

Area Bishops - *Horsham*, R. K. F. Bushyager, MSci, BA; *Lewes*, W. P. G. Hazlewood, BA, BTh

Dean - S. J. Waine

Archdeacons - *Chichester*, L. T. Irvine-Capel, BA, MA; *Horsham*, A. F. Martin; *Hastings*, R. E. M. Dowler, BA, PhD; *Brighton and Lewes*, M. C. Lloyd Williams, BEd

Diocesan Secretary - G. Higgins, Diocesan Church House, 211 New Church Road, Hove, East Sussex, BN3 4ED. Tel: 01273 421021 email: Diocesan.Secretary@chichester.anglican.org

Coventry www.coventry.anglican.org

Bishop - C. J. Cocksworth, BA, PGCE, PhD [*Bishop's House, 23 Davenport Road, Coventry, CV5 6PW*] [Christopher Coventry]

Suffragan Bishop - *Warwick*, J. R. A. Stroyan, MTheol, MA, PhD

Dean - J. J. Witcombe, MA, MPhil

Archdeacons - *Archdeacon Pastor*, S. E. Field, BA, CertEd, MTh; *Archdeacon Missioner*, B. J. Dugmore

Diocesan Secretary - J. Ladds, Cathedral and Diocesan Offices, 1 Hill Top, Coventry, CV1 5AB. Tel: 024 7652 1307 email: jacqueline.ladds@coventry.anglican.org

Derby https://derby.anglican.org

Bishop - E. J. H. Lane, BA, MA [*The Bishop's Office, 6 King Street, Duffield, DE56 4EU*] [Libby Derby]

Suffragan Bishop - *Repton*, W. M. Macnaughton, BA

Dean - P. J. A. Robinson, BA, MA, PhD

Archdeacons - *Derbyshire Peak & Dales*, C. A. Coslett, BD, PGCE, MA; *Derby City & South Derbyshire*, M. J. H. Trick, BSc, BTh; *East Derbyshire*, K. E. Hamblin, BA, PGCE

Diocesan Secretary - M. Marples (*Acting*), Derby Church House, Full Street, Derby, DE1 3DR. Tel: 01332 388650 email: martyn.marples@derby.anglican.org

Ely www.elydiocese.org

Bishop - S. D. Conway, BA, MA, CertEd [*The Bishop's House, Ely, CB7 4DW*] [Stephen Ely]

Suffragan Bishop - *Huntingdon*, D. Winter, Dr Theol

Dean - M. P. J. Bonney, BA, MA

Archdeacons - *Cambridge*, A. J. Hughes, BA, MA, MPhil, PhD; *Huntingdon and Wisbech*, R. J. St C. Harlow, BA, MA

Diocesan Secretary - P. L. Evans, Diocesan Office, Bishop Woodford House, Barton Road, Ely, CB7 4DX. Tel: 01353 652701 email: paul.evans@elydiocese.org

Europe (Diocese in Europe) https://europe.anglican.org

Bishop - R. N. Innes, BA, MA, PhD [*Office of the Bishop of Gibraltar in Europe, 47 rue Capitaine Crespel - boîte 49, 1050 Brussels, Belgium*] [Robert Gibraltar in Europe]

Suffragan Bishop in Europe - D. Hamid, BSc, MDiv, Hon DD

Archdeacons - *Eastern, Germany and Northern Europe*, L. Nathaniel; *France and Switzerland*, P. G. Hooper, BSc, PhD; *Gibraltar, Italy and Malta*, D. J. Waller, BA, MA, MTh; *North West Europe*, S. W. Van Leer, BA, MA (*Acting*)

Diocesan Secretary - A. Caspari, 14 Tufton Street, London, SW1P 3QZ. Tel: 020 7898 1156
email: andrew.caspari@churchofengland.org

Exeter https://exeter.anglican.org

Bishop - R. R. Atwell, BA, MLitt [*The Palace, Exeter, EX1 1HY*] [Robert Exon]

Suffragan Bishops - *Crediton*, J. A. Searle, BEd, MA; *Plymouth*, J. E. Grier, BA, MA

Dean - J. D. F. Greener, BA, MA

Archdeacons - *Exeter*, A. M. Beane, BA; *Plymouth*, N. S. Shutt, BA, LLB, LLM; *Barnstaple*, V. Breed; *Totnes*, D. J. Dettmer, BA, MDiv

Diocesan Secretary - S. Hancock, The Old Deanery, The Cloisters, Exeter, EX1 1HS. Tel: 01392 294927 email: stephen.hancock@exeter.anglican.org

Gloucester www.gloucester.anglican.org

Bishop - R. Treweek, BA, BTh [*2 College Green, Gloucester, GL1 2LR*] [Rachel Gloucester]

Suffragan Bishop - *Tewkesbury*, R. W. Springett, BTh, MA

Dean - A. J. Braddock, BA, MA, PhD (*Interim*)

Archdeacons - *Cheltenham*, P. J. Andrew, BSc, MTh; *Gloucester*, H. J. Dawson, BA, PGCE, MA

Diocesan Secretary - B. Preece Smith, Church House, 6 College Green, Gloucester, GL1 2LY. Tel: 01452 835523 email: bpreecesmith@glosdioc.org.uk

Guildford www.cofeguildford.org.uk

Bishop - A. J. Watson, BA, MA [*Willow Grange, Woking Road, Guildford, GU4 7QS*] [Andrew Guildford]

Suffragan Bishop - *Dorking* (*Vacant*)

Dean - D. L. Gwilliams, BA, MA

Archdeacons - *Surrey*, R. P. Davies, BA, MTh; *Dorking*, M. C. Breadmore, LLB, BTh

Diocesan Secretary - S. Collins (*Acting*), Church House, 20 Alan Turing Road, Guildford, GU2 7YF. Tel: 01483 790301 email: steve.collins@cofeguildford.org.uk

Hereford www.hereford.anglican.org

Bishop - R. C. Jackson, BA, MSc [*The Bishop's House, The Palace, Hereford, HR4 9BN*] [Richard Hereford]

Dean - S. Brown

Archdeacons - *Hereford*, D. C. Chedzey, BA, MA; *Ludlow*, F. R. Gibson, BEd, MTh

Diocesan Secretary - S. Pratley, The Diocesan Office, The Palace, Hereford, HR4 9BL. Tel: 01432 373314 email: s.pratley@hereford.anglican.org

Leicester www.leicester.anglican.org

Bishop - M. J. Snow, BSc, BTh [*Bishop's Lodge, 12 Springfield Road, Leicester, LE2 3BD*] [Martyn Leicester]

Suffragan Bishop - *Loughborough*, V. M. L. Muthalaly, BTh

Dean - K. S. F. Rooms, BA, MTh (*Acting*)

Archdeacons - *Leicester*, R. V. Worsfold, LLB, BA; *Loughborough*, C. Wood

Diocesan Secretary - J. W. Kerry, St Martin's House, 7 Peacock Lane, Leicester, LE1 5PZ. Tel: 0116 261 5326 email: jonathan.kerry@leicestercofe.org

Lichfield www.lichfield.anglican.org

Bishop - M. G. Ipgrave, OBE, BA, MA, PhD [*The Bishop's House, 22 The Close, Lichfield, WS13 7LG*] [Michael Lichfield]

Area Bishops - *Shrewsbury*, S. R. Bullock, BA; *Stafford*, M. J. Parker, BA, MA; *Wolverhampton*, C. M. Gregory, BA, MA, Hon MA

Dean - A. J. Dorber, BA, MTh

Archdeacons - *Lichfield*, S. K. Weller, BSc, PhD, BA; *Salop*, P. W. Thomas, BA, BTh, MA; *Stoke*, M. R. Smith, MBChB, MTh, MSc, MRCP, FHEA, FRCPCH; *Walsall*, J. M. Francis, BA, MA

Chief Executive Officer and Diocesan Secretary - J. Jones, St Mary's House, The Close, Lichfield, WS13 7LD. Tel: 01543 306291 email: julie.jones@lichfield.anglican.org

Lincoln www.lincoln.anglican.org

Bishop - S. D. Conway, BA, MA, CertEd (*Acting*) [*Edward King House, Minster Yard, Lincoln, LN2 1PU*]

Suffragan Bishops - *Grimsby*, D. E. Court, BA, BSc, PGCE, PhD; *Grantham*, N. A. Chamberlain, BA, BD, PhD

Dean - C. L. Wilson

Archdeacons - *Boston*, J. P. H. Allain Chapman, BA, PGCE, MDiv, DThMin, AKC; *Lincoln*, G. J. Kirk, BTh, MA, LLM; *Stow and Lindsey*, A. C. Buxton

Diocesan Secretary - D. I. Dadswell, Edward King House, Minster Yard, Lincoln, LN2 1PU. Tel: 01522 504032 email: David.dadswell@lincoln.anglican.org

Norwich www.dioceseofnorwich.org

Bishop - G. B. Usher, BSc, BA, MA [*Bishop's House, Norwich, NR3 1SB*] [Graham Norwich]

Suffragan Bishops - *Thetford*, A. P. Winton, BA, PhD; *Lynn*, J. E. Steen, BA, MA, PhD, LLM

Dean - A. J. Braddock, BA, MA, PhD

Archdeacons - *Norwich*, K. N. James, BA, MA; *Lynn*, C. H. Dobson; *Norfolk*, S. J. Betts, BSc

Diocesan Secretary - T. Sweeting, Diocesan House, 109 Dereham Road, Easton, Norwich, NR9 5ES. Tel: 01603 880853 email: tim.sweeting@dioceseofnorwich.org

Oxford www.oxford.anglican.org

Bishop - S. J. L. Croft, BA, MA, PhD [*Church House Oxford, Langford Locks, Kidlington, Oxford, OX5 1GF*] [Steven Oxon]

Area Bishops - *Dorchester*, G. A. Collins, BA, MA; *Reading*, D. J. Graham, BA; *Buckingham*, A. T. L. Wilson, BA, MA, DPhil

Dean of Christ Church - (*Vacant*)

Archdeacons - *Oxford*, J. P. M. Chaffey; *Buckingham*, G. C. Elsmore, BSc; *Berkshire*, S. J. Pullin, BA, BEng, MBA; *Dorchester*, D. S. Tyler, BSc, ACA

Diocesan Secretary - M. Humphriss, Church House Oxford, Langford Locks, Kidlington, Oxford, OX5 1GF. Tel: 01865 208202 email: diocesan.secretary@oxford.anglican.org

Queen's Free Chapel of St George, Windsor Castle www.stgeorges-windsor.org

Dean - D. J. Conner, BA, MA, KCVO

Peterborough www.peterborough-diocese.org.uk

Bishop - D. S. Allister, BA, MA, Hon DTh [*The Bishop's Lodging, The Palace, Peterborough, PE1 1YA*] [Donald Petriburg]

Suffragan Bishop - *Brixworth*, J. E. Holbrook, BA, MA

Dean - C. C. Dalliston, BA, MA

Archdeacons - *Northampton*, R. J. Ormston, BA, MTh; *Oakham*, A. S. W. Booker, BA, MA

Diocesan Secretary - A. Roberts, Diocesan Office, The Palace, Peterborough, PE1 1YB. Tel: 01733 887002 email: diosec@peterborough-diocese.org.uk

Portsmouth www.portsmouth.anglican.org

Bishop - J. H. Frost, BD, MTh, DUniv, MSSTh [*Bishopsgrove, 26 Osborn Road, Fareham, PO16 7DQ*] [Jonathan Portsmouth]

Dean - A. W. N. S. Cane, BA, MPhil, PhD

Archdeacons - *Portsdown*, J. J. E. Rowley; *The Meon*, W. P. M. Hughes, BA (*Acting*); *Isle of Wight*, S. J. Daughtery, BSc, BA

Diocesan Secretary - (*Vacant*), Diocese of Portsmouth, First Floor, Peninsular House, Wharf Road, Portsmouth, PO2 8HB. Tel: 02392 899655 email: via website

Rochester www.rochester.anglican.org

Bishop - J. Gibbs [*Bishopscourt, 24 St Margaret's Street, Rochester, ME1 1TS*] [Jonathan Roffen]

Suffragan Bishop - *Tonbridge*, S. D. Burton-Jones, BA, BTh, MA

Dean - P. J. Hesketh, BD, PhD, AKC

Archdeacons - *Rochester*, A. D. Wooding Jones, BA, MBA; *Tonbridge*, S. L. Copestake, BA; *Bromley and Bexley*, A. Kerr

Diocesan Secretary - M. Girt, Diocesan Office, St Nicholas Church, Boley Hill, Rochester, ME1 1SL. Tel: 01634 560000 email: matthew.girt@rochester.anglican.org

St Albans www.stalbans.anglican.org

Bishop - A. G. C. Smith, BA, MA, PhD, HonDD [*Abbey Gate House, 4 Abbey Mill Lane, St Albans, AL3 4HD*] [Alan St Albans]

Suffragan Bishops - *Hertford*, J. Mainwaring, BA, MPhil, PhD (*Elect*); *Bedford*, R. W. B. Atkinson, OBE, MA

Dean - J. Kelly-Moore, BA, LLB, BD

Archdeacons - *St Albans* (*Vacant*); *Bedford*, D. J. Middlebrook, BA, BSc, MSc; *Hertford*, J. Mackenzie, BEd, BA

Diocesan Secretary - D. White, Diocesan Office, Holywell Lodge, 41 Holywell Hill, St Albans, AL1 1HE. Tel: 01727 818131 email: dwhite@stalbans.anglican.org

St Edmundsbury and Ipswich www.cofesuffolk.org

Bishop - M. A. Seeley, BA, MA [*The Bishop's House, 4 Park Road, Ipswich, IP1 3ST*] [Martin St Eds and Ips]

Suffragan Bishop - Dunwich, M. R. Harrison, BA, MA, PhD

Dean - J. P. Hawes, BA, MA

Archdeacons - Ipswich, R. E. King, BA, MA; *Sudbury*, D. H. Jenkins, BA, MA, PhD; *Suffolk*, J. M. Gosney, BA, PGCE, BTh, MPhil, MA; *Rural Mission*, S. A. Gaze, BA, MA, MPhil, PGCE

Diocesan Secretary - G. Bultitude, Diocesan Office, St Nicholas Centre, 4 Cutler Street, Ipswich, IP1 1UQ. Tel: 01473 298500 email: gavin.bultitude@cofesuffolk.org

Salisbury www.salisbury.anglican.org

Bishop - S. D. Lake, BTh [*South Canonry, 71 The Close, Salisbury, SP1 2ER*] [Stephen Sarum]

Area Bishops - Sherborne, K. M. Gorham, BA; *Ramsbury*, A. P. Rumsey, BA, MA, DThMin

Dean - N. C. Papadopulos, BA, MA

Archdeacons - Sherborne, P. J. Sayer, BA; *Dorset*, A. C. MacRow-Wood, BA, ACA; *Sarum*, A. P. Jeans, BTh, MA, MIAAS, MIBCO; *Wilts*, S. A. Groom, BA, MPhil, MA, DThM

Diocesan Secretary - D. Pain, Church House, Crane Street, Salisbury, SP1 2QB. Tel: 01722 411922 email: david.pain@salisbury.anglican.org

Southwark https://southwark.anglican.org

Bishop - C. T. J. Chessun, BA, MA [*Bishop's House, 38 Tooting Bec Gardens, London, SW16 1QZ*] [Christopher Southwark]

Area Bishops - Kingston-upon-Thames, J. M. Gainsborough, MA, MSc, PhD (*Elect*); *Woolwich*, W. K. Dorgu, MBBS, BA, MA; *Croydon*, M. R. Mallett, BA, PhD

Dean - A. P. Nunn, BA

Archdeacons - Lewisham and Greenwich, A. M. Cutting, BEd, MA; *Southwark*, J. E. Steen, BA, MA, PhD; *Lambeth*, S. P. Gates, MA, BA; *Wandsworth*, J. Kiddle, BA, MA, MTh; *Reigate*, M. A. E. Astin, BA, MA; *Croydon*, G. S. Prior, BTh

Diocesan Secretary - R. Martin, DipHE, BA, MA, Southwark Diocesan Office, Trinity House, 4 Chapel Court, Borough High Street, London, SE1 1HW. Tel: 020 7939 9400 email: via website

Truro https://trurodiocese.org.uk

Bishop - P. I. Mounstephen, BA, MA, PGCE [*Lis Escop, Feock, Truro, TR3 6QQ*] [Philip Truro]

Suffragan Bishop - St Germans, H. E. Nelson, BA

Dean - S. J. Robinson, BA (*Interim*)

Archdeacons - Bodmin, K. A. Betteridge, BA, MA; *Cornwall*, P. D. Bryer, BEd, MA

Diocesan Secretary - S. P. V. Cade, BA, Church House, Woodlands Court, Truro Business Park, Threemilestone, Truro, TR4 9NH. Tel: 07517 100676 email: simon.cade@truro.anglican.org

Worcester www.cofe-worcester.org.uk

Bishop - J. G. Inge, BSc, MA, PGCE, PhD [*The Bishop's Office, The Old Palace, Deansway, Worcester, WR1 2JE*] [John Wigorn]

Suffragan Bishop - Dudley, M. C. W. Gorick, BA, MA

Dean - P. G. Atkinson, BA, MA, Hon DLitt, FRSA

Archdeacons - Worcester, R. G. Jones, BA, MA; *Dudley*, N. J. Groarke, BA

Diocesan Secretary - J. Preston, Diocesan Office, 16 Lowesmoor Wharf, Worcester, WR1 2RS. Tel: 01905 732801 email: jpreston@cofe-worcester.org.uk

Provincial Episcopal Visitors in the Province of Canterbury

Bishop of Ebbsfleet - R. S. Munro, BSc, PGCE, BA, DMin

Bishop of Maidstone (*Vacant*)

Bishop of Oswestry - P. Thomas, BA, MA, Hon ARAM

Bishop of Richborough - N. Banks, BA, MA, Parkside House, Abbey Mill Lane, St Albans, AL3 4HE. Tel: 01727 836358

Province of York

York https://dioceseofyork.org.uk

Archbishop - S. G. Cottrell, BA, MA. Primate of England and Metropolitan [*Bishopthorpe Palace, York, YO23 2GE*] [Stephen Ebor]

Suffragan Bishops - *Beverley*, S. P. Race, BA, MTh; *Selby*, J. B. Thomson, BA, MA, PhD; *Hull*, E. R. Sanderson, BSc, MA, PhD, MTh; *Whitby*, P. J. Ferguson, BA, MA, FRCO

Dean - D. M. J. Barrington, BA, MSc, LTCL, MTS, MA

Archdeacons - *York*, S. J. Rushton, BA, MA; *East Riding*, A. C. Broom, BSocSc, BA; *Cleveland*, A. E. Bloor, BA, MA, PhD, PGCE

Diocesan Secretary and Chief Executive - P. J. Warry, BSc, The Diocese of York, Amy Johnson House, Amy Johnson Way, York, YO30 4XT. Tel: 01904 699500 email: office@yorkdiocese.org

Durham https://durhamdiocese.org

Bishop - P. R. Butler, BA [*The Bishop of Durham's Office, Auckland Castle, Market Place, Bishop Auckland, DL14 7NR*] [Paul Dunelm]

Suffragan Bishop - *Jarrow*, S. E. Clark, BA, MBA, MA

Dean (*Vacant*)

Provost of Sunderland Minster (*Vacant*)

Archdeacons - *Sunderland*, R. G. Cooper, BD; *Durham*, E. M. Wilkinson, MA; *Auckland*, R. L. Simpson, BA, MPhil, PGCE

Diocesan Secretary and Secretary to the Board of Finance - J. Morgan, Diocesan Office, Cuthbert House, Stonebridge, Durham, DH1 3RY. Tel: 07436 213127 email: james.morgan@durham.anglican.org

Blackburn www.blackburn.anglican.org

Bishop - P. J. North, BA, MA (*Acting*) [*Bishop's House, Ribchester Road, Clayton-le-Dale, Blackburn, BB1 9EF*]

Suffragan Bishops - *Lancaster*, J. L. C. Duff, BA, MA, DPhil; *Burnley*, P. J. North, BA, MA

Dean - P. Howell-Jones, BMus, PGCE

Archdeacons - *Blackburn*, M. C. Ireland, MTheol, MA; *Lancaster*, D. A. Picken, BA, MA, PGCE

Diocesan Secretary - S. Whittaker (*Acting*), Diocesan Offices, Clayton House, Walker Industrial Estate, Walker Road, Blackburn, BB1 2QE. Tel: 01254 503404 email: stephen.whittaker@blackburn.anglican.org

Carlisle www.carlislediocese.org.uk

Bishop - J. W. S. Newcome, BA, MA [*Bishop's House, Ambleside Road, Keswick, CA12 4DD*] [James Carliol]

Suffragan Bishop - *Penrith*, R. Saner-Haigh, BA, MPhil, MA

Dean (*Vacant*)

Archdeacons - *Carlisle* (*Vacant*); *West Cumberland*, S. J. Fyfe, BSc; *Westmorland and Furness*, V. Ross, BSc, RGN, MA

Diocesan Secretary - D. Hurton, Church House, 19-24 Friargate, Penrith, Cumbria, CA11 7XR. Tel: 01768 807760 email: derek.hurton@carlislediocese.org.uk

Chester www.chester.anglican.org

Bishop - M. S. A. Tanner, BA, MA, MTh [*Bishop's House, 1 Abbey Street, Chester, CH1 2JD*] [Mark Cestr]

Suffragan Bishops - *Birkenhead*, J. A. Conalty; *Stockport*, S. J. C. Corley, BA, MA, PGCE

Dean - T. R. Stratford, BSc, PhD

Archdeacons - *Chester*, M. R. Gilbertson, BA, MA, PhD; *Macclesfield*, I. G. Bishop, BSc, MRICS, BA

Diocesan Secretary - G. Colville, Chester Diocesan Board of Finance, Church House, 5500 Daresbury Park, Daresbury, Warrington, WA4 4GE. Tel: 01928 718834 ext 247 email: george.colville@chester.anglican.org

Leeds www.leeds.anglican.org

Bishop - N. Baines, BA [*Hollin House, Weetwood Avenue, Leeds, LS16 5NG*] [Nicholas Leeds]

Area Bishops - *Bradford*, T. M. Howarth, BA, MA, PhD; *Huddersfield* (*Vacant*); *Kirkstall*, A. Arora, LLB, BA; *Ripon* (*Vacant*); *Wakefield*, A. W. Robinson, CertEd

Deans - *Bradford*, A. M. Bowerman, BSc, MSW, MA; *Ripon*, J. R. Dobson, BA; *Wakefield*, S. C. Cowling, BA, MA, PGCE

Archdeacons - *Bradford*, A. J. Jolley, BSc, BTh, CEng, MIMechE, MBA, PhD; *Huddersfield*, W. E. Braviner, BSc, BA, MA, ACA, FCA; *Leeds*, P. N. Ayers, BA, MA; *Pontefract*, P. K. Townley, BA; *Richmond and Craven*, J. R. B. Gough, BA, MTh, FRSA

Diocesan Secretary - J. Wood, Church House, 17-19 York Place, Leeds, LS1 2EX. Tel: 0113 353 0303 email: jonathan.wood@leeds.anglican.org

Liverpool www.liverpool.anglican.org

Bishop - J. Perumbalath, BA, BD, MA, PhD [*Bishop's Lodge, Woolton Park, Liverpool, L25 6DT*] [John Liverpool]

Suffragan Bishop - *Warrington*, B. A. Mason, BA

Dean - S. H. Jones, BEd, MPhil, PhD

Archdeacons - *Knowsley and Sefton*, P. H. Spiers, BA; *Liverpool* (*Vacant*); *St Helens and Warrington*, J. P. Fisher, BA; *Wigan and West Lancashire* (*Vacant*)

Diocesan Secretary - M. J. Eastwood, St James' House, 20 St James Road, Liverpool, L1 7BY. Tel: 0151 705 2112 email: mike.eastwood@liverpool.anglican.org

Manchester www.manchester.anglican.org

Bishop - D. S. Walker, MA, PhD [*Bishopscourt, Bury New Road, Salford, M7 4LE*] [David Manchester]

Suffragan Bishops - *Bolton*, M. D. Ashcroft, BA, MA; *Middleton*, M. Davies, BA

Dean - R. M. Govender, MBE, BTh

Archdeacons - *Manchester*, K. B. Lund; *Rochdale*, D. J. Sharples, BD, AKC; *Bolton and Salford*, J. A. Burgess, MA

Chief Operating Officer and Diocesan Secretary - H. Platts, Church House, 90 Deansgate, M3 2GH. Tel: 0161 828 1400 email: helenplatts@manchester.anglican.org

Newcastle www.newcastle.anglican.org

Bishop - H.-A. M. Hartley, MTheol, ThM, MPhil, DPhil [*Bishop's House, 29 Moor Road South, Gosforth, Newcastle upon Tyne, NE3 1PA*]

Suffragan Bishop - *Berwick*, M. Wroe, BA, MA

Dean - G. V. Miller, BEd, MA

Archdeacons - *Lindisfarne*, C. A. Sourbut Groves, BA, MSc, PhD; *Northumberland*, R. A. Wood, BA, MA

Diocesan Secretary - S. Waddle, Church House, St John's Terrace, North Shields, NE29 6HS. Tel: 0191 270 4114 email: s.waddle@newcastle.anglican.org

Sheffield www.sheffield.anglican.org

Bishop - P. J. Wilcox, BA, MA, DPhil [*Bishopscroft, Snaithing Lane, Sheffield, S10 3LG*] [Pete Sheffield]

Suffragan Bishop - *Doncaster*, S. R. Jelley, BA, MPhil

Dean - A. L. Thompson, BMus, BA

Archdeacons - *Sheffield and Rotherham*, M. L. Chamberlain; BA, BTh, MPhil; *Doncaster*, J. Iqbal, BA, MA

Diocesan Secretary - K. Bell, Church House, 95–99 Effingham Street, Rotherham, S65 1BL. Tel: 01709 309100 email: katie.bell@sheffield.anglican.org

Sodor and Man www.sodorandman.im

Bishop - P. A. Eagles, BA, AKC [*Thie yn Aspick, 4 The Falls, Douglas, Isle of Man, IM4 4PZ*] [Peter Sodor and Man]

Dean - N. P. Godfrey, BA, MA, MBA, MSc

Archdeacon of Man - I. C. Cowell, RGN

Diocesan Secretary, T. Connell email: via website

Southwell and Nottingham https://southwell.anglican.org

Bishop - P. G. Williams, BA [*Bishop's Manor, Southwell, NG25 0JR*] [Paul Southwell]

Suffragan Bishop - *Sherwood*, A. N. Emerton, BSc, DPhil, BTh

Dean - N. A. Sullivan, SRN, RM, BTh

Archdeacons - *Nottingham*, P. A. Williams, BA; *Newark*, V. C. Ramsey

Diocesan Chief Executive - M. Cooper, Jubilee House, 8 Westgate, Southwell, NG25 0JH. Tel: 01636 817206 email: ce@southwell.anglican.org

Provincial Episcopal Visitor in the Province of York

Bishop of Beverley - S. P. Race, BA, MTh [*The Bishop of Beverley's Office, Holy Trinity Rectory, Micklegate, York, YO1 6LE*] [Stephen Beverley]

The Church in Wales

St Asaph https://dioceseofstasaph.org.uk

Bishop - G. K. Cameron, BA, MA, MPhil, LLM [*Esgobty, Upper Denbigh Road, St Asaph, LL17 0TW*] [Gregory Llanelwy]

Dean - N. H. Williams

Archdeacons - *St Asaph*, A. S. Grimwood, BA, BD; *Montgomery*, B. F. Wilson, BA, MPhil, MTh, PGCE; *Wrexham* (*Vacant*)

Diocesan Secretary - D. McCarthy, Diocesan Office, High Street, St Asaph, Denbighshire, LL17 0RD. Tel: 01745 582245 email: dianemccarthy@cinw.org.uk

Bangor https://bangor.eglwysyngnghymru.org.uk

Bishop - A. T. G. John, LLB, BA [*Tŷ'r Esgob, Upper Garth Road, Bangor, LL57 2SS*] [Andrew Bangor]

Assistant Bishop - M. K. R. Stallard, BA, PGCE

Dean (*Vacant*)

Archdeacons - *Bangor*, M. K. R. Stallard, BA, PGCE; *Meirionydd*, A. Jones, BD, BTh, PGCE, MA, MPhil; *Anglesey*, J. C. Harvey, BA, BTh

Diocesan Secretary - S. R. Evans, The Diocesan Centre, Cathedral Close, Bangor, Tŷ Deiniol, LL57 1RL. Tel: 01248 354999 email: sionrhysevans@churchinwales.org.uk

Llandaff https://llandaff.churchinwales.org.uk

Bishop - J. Osborne, BA [*Llys Esgob, The Cathedral Green, Llandaff, Cardiff, CF5 2YE*] [June Llandaff]

Dean - R. C. Peers, BEd, BTh, MA

Archdeacons - *Llandaff*, R. E. A. Green, BA, MA; *Margam*, M. Komor, BSc

Diocesan Secretary - J. Laing, The Diocesan Office, The Court, Coychurch, Bridgend, CF35 5EH. Tel: 01656 868864 email: jameslaing@churchinwales.org.uk

Monmouth https://monmouth.churchinwales.org.uk

Bishop - C. E. Vann, ARCM, GRSM [*Bishopstow, Stow Hill, Newport, NP20 4EA*] [Elizabeth Monmouth]

Dean - I. C. Black, BA, MDiv

Archdeacons - *Newport*, J. S. Williams, BSc; *Monmouth*, I. K. Rees; *Gwent Valleys*, S. Bailey, BTheol

Diocesan Secretary - I. Thompson, Monmouth Diocesan Office, 64 Caerau Road, Newport, NP20 4HJ. Tel: 01633 267490 email: isabelthompson@churchinwales.org.uk

St Davids https://stdavids.churchinwales.org.uk

Bishop - J. S. Penberthy, BA, MA, MTh [*Llys Esgob, Abergwili, Carmarthen, SA31 2JG*] [Joanna Tyddewi]

Dean - S. C. Rowland Jones, LVO, OBE, BA, MA

Archdeacons - *Carmarthen*, D. P. Davies, BA; *Cardigan*, R. H. E. Davies, MBE, BTh; *St Davids*, P. R. Mackness, BA

Diocesan Secretary - H. Llewellyn, Diocesan Office, Abergwili, Carmarthen, SA31 2JG. Tel: 01267 236145 email: howardllewellyn@churchinwales.org.uk

Swansea and Brecon https://swanseaandbrecon.churchinwales.org.uk

Archbishop of Wales and Bishop of Swansea and Brecon, J. D. P. Lomas [*Ely Tower, Castle Square, Brecon, LD3 9DJ*] [John Swansea and Brecon]

Dean of Brecon Cathedral - A. P. Shakerley, MA, PhD

Archdeacons - *Brecon*, A. N. Jevons, BA, MA; *Gower*, J. B. Davies, BTh

Diocesan Secretary - L. Pearson, Diocesan Centre, Cathedral Close, Brecon, Powys, LD3 9DP. Tel: 01874 623716 email: louisepearson@churchinwales.org.uk

The Episcopal Church in Scotland

www.scotland.anglican.org

Aberdeen and Orkney aoepiscopal.scot

Bishop - J. A. Armes, BA, MA, PhD (*Acting*) [*Ashley House, 16 Ashley Gardens, Aberdeen, AB10 6RQ*]

Dean - D. B. A. Berk, BA, MDiv, DMin

Provost of St Andrew's Cathedral, Aberdeen - I. M. Poobalan, RGN, BD, MTh, MPhil

Diocesan Secretary - E. Finlayson, The Diocese of Aberdeen and Orkney, University of Aberdeen, Marischal College, Broad Street, Aberdeen, AB10 1YS email: office@aberdeen.anglican.org

Argyll and the Isles https://argyll.anglican.org

Bishop - K. G. Riglin, BEd, BA, MA, MTh, ThD, FRSA, AKC, MSSTh [*St Moluag's Diocesan Centre, Croft Avenue, Oban, PA34 5JJ*] [Keith Argyll and the Isles]

Dean - M. R. Campbell, BA

Provost of St John's Cathedral, Oban - M. R. Campbell, BA

Diocesan Secretary - H. Hardstaff, St Moluag's Diocesan Centre, Croft Avenue, Oban, PA34 5JJ. Tel: 01631 570870 email: secretary@argyll.anglican.org

Brechin www.thedioceseofbrechin.org

Bishop - A. C. Swift, BEng, MSc, BTh [*Bishop's House, 5 Ballumbie View, Dundee, DD4 0NQ*] [Andrew Brechin]

Dean - E. M. Lamont, BA

Provost of St Paul's Cathedral, Dundee - E. J. Thomson, MA, DPhil, BA, PGCE

Diocesan Secretary - M. Duncan, Diocesan Centre, 38 Langlands Street, Dundee, DD4 6SZ. Tel: 07444 161300 email: diosec@brechin.anglican.org

Edinburgh https://edinburgh.anglican.org

Bishop - J. A. Armes, BA, MA, PhD [*Bishop's Office, 21a Grosvenor Crescent, Edinburgh, EH12 5EL*] [John Edenburgen]

Dean - F. S. Burberry, ACII

Provost of St Mary's Cathedral, Edinburgh - J. A. Conway, BEng, BD

Diocesan Secretary - G. Robson, The Diocese of Edinburgh, 21a Grosvenor Crescent, Edinburgh, EH12 5EL. Tel: 0131 538 7033 email: diosec@dioceseofedinburgh.anglican.org

Glasgow and Galloway https://glasgow.anglican.org

Bishop - K. Pearson, BA, BD [*Bishop's Office, Diocesan Centre, 5 St Vincent Place, Glasgow, G1 2DH*]

Dean - R. J. Preston, BSc, MEng, MA, PGCE

Provost of St Mary's Cathedral, Glasgow - K. Holdsworth, BSc, BD, MTh

Diocesan Secretary - J. Mitchell, Glasgow and Galloway Diocesan Centre, 5 St Vincent Place, Glasgow, G1 2DH. email: office@glasgow.anglican.org

Moray, Ross and Caithness https://morayepiscopalchurch.scot

Bishop, Primus of the Scottish Episcopal Church - M. J. Strange, LTh [*Bishop's House, St John's, Arpafeelie, North Kessock, Inverness, IV1 3XD*] [Mark Moray, Ross and Caithness]

Dean - A. J. Simpson, BSc, BD, MTh

Provost, St Andrew's Cathedral, Inverness - S. E. Murray, BTh

Diocesan Secretary - I. Foyers, The United Diocese of Moray, Ross and Caithness, 9-11 Kenneth Street, Inverness, IV3 5NR. Tel: 01463 237503 email: diocesansecretary@moray.anglican.org

St Andrews, Dunkeld and Dunblane https://standrews.anglican.org

Bishop - I. J. Paton, MA, PGCE, MTh [*Diocesan Office, 28a Balhousie Street, Perth, PH1 5HJ*] [Ian St Andrews]

Dean - G. S. Taylor

Provost of St Ninian's Cathedral, Perth - H. B. Farquharson, ALAM, LLAM

Diocesan Secretary (*Vacant*), The Diocese of St Andrews, Dunkeld and Dunblane, 28a Balhousie Street, Perth, PH1 5HJ. Tel: 01738 443173 email: bishopsec@standrews.anglican.org

The Church of Ireland

Province of Armagh

Armagh www.armagh.anglican.org

Archbishop - F. J. McDowell, BA, BTh, Primate of All Ireland and Metropolitan [*Church House, 46 Abbey Street, Armagh, BT61 7DZ*] [John Armagh]

Dean - T. S. Forster, BA, BTh, MPhil

Diocesan Secretary – J. Leighton, Church House, 46 Abbey Street, Armagh, BT61 7DZ. Tel: 028 3752 2858 email: secretary@armagh.anglican.org

Clogher https://clogher.anglican.org

Bishop – I. W. Ellis, BSc, CertEd, EdD, BTh [*The See House, Ballagh Road, Fivemiletown, Co. Tyrone, BT75 0QP*] [Ian Clogher]

Dean – K. R. J. Hall

Diocesan Secretary – G. M. T. Moore, Clogher Diocesan Office, St Macartin's Cathedral Hall, Halls Lane, Enniskillen, Co. Fermanagh, BT74 7DR. Tel: 028 6634 7879 email: secretary@clogher.anglican.org

Connor https://connor.anglican.org

Bishop – G. T. W. Davison, BD, BTh [*Bishop's House, 27 Grange Road, Doagh, Ballyclare, BT39 0RQ*] [George Connor]

Deans – *Connor*, W. S. Wright, BTh, MA; *Belfast*, S. Forde, BSc, DipTh

Diocesan Secretary (*Vacant*), Connor Diocesan Office, Church of Ireland House, 61–67 Donegall Street, Belfast, BT1 2QH. Tel: 028 9082 8830 email: office@connordiocese.org

Derry and Raphoe https://derryandraphoe.org

Bishop – A. J. Forster, BA, BTh [*Diocesan Office, 24 London Street, Londonderry, BT48 6RQ*] [Andrew Derry and Raphoe]

Deans – *Derry*, R. J. Stewart, BA, MA; *Raphoe* (*Vacant*)

Diocesan Secretary (*Vacant*), The Diocesan Office, 24 London Street, Londonderry, BT48 6RQ. Tel: 028 7126 2440 email: via website

Down and Dromore www.downanddromore.org

Bishop – D. A. McClay [*The See House, 32 Knockdene Park South, Belfast, BT5 7AB*] [David Down and Dromore]

Deans – *Down*, T. H. Hull, BD; *Dromore*, S. G. Wilson, BTh

Diocesan Secretary – R. Lawther, Church of Ireland House, 61–67 Donegall Street, Belfast, BT1 2QH. Tel: 028 9082 8830 email: rlawther@downdromorediocese.org

Kilmore, Elphin and Ardagh www.dkea.ie

Bishop – S. F. Glenfield, BA, MLitt, MA, MTh [*The See House, Kilmore Upper, Cavan, Co. Cavan, H16 TV29*] [Ferran Kilmore]

Deans – *Kilmore*, N. N. Crossey, BA; *Elphin and Ardagh*, A. Williams, BD, MA

Diocesan Secretary (*Vacant*), Diocesan Office, 20A Market Street, Cootehill, Co. Cavan, H16 XT02. Tel: 049 555 9954 email: secretary@kilmore.anglican.org

Province of Dublin

Dublin and Glendalough https://dublin.anglican.org

Archbishop – M. G. St A. Jackson, BA, MA, PhD, DPhil, Primate of Ireland and Metropolitan [*The See House, 17 Temple Road, Dartry, Dublin 6*] [Michael Dublin and Glendalough]

Dean – D. P. M. Dunne, BA, MA

Diocesan and Glebes Secretary – S. Heggie, United Dioceses of Dublin and Glendalough, Church of Ireland House, Church Avenue, Rathmines, Dublin 6, D06 CF67. Tel: 01 496 6981 email: admin@dublin.anglican.org and via website

National Cathedral and Collegiate Church of St Patrick, Dublin 8 www.stpatrickscathedral.ie

Dean and Ordinary – W. W. Morton, BTh, MA, MMus, PhD

Meath and Kildare https://meathandkildare.org

Bishop – P. L. Storey, MA, BTh [*Bishop's House, Moyglare, Maynooth, Co. Kildare, W23 NK55*] [Pat Meath and Kildare]

Deans - *Clonmacnoise*, P. D. Bogle, BTh; *Kildare*, T. Wright, BSc, MTh

Diocesan Secretary - K. Seaman, Meath and Kildare Diocesan Centre, Moyglare, Maynooth, Co. Kildare, W23 WK76. Tel: 01 629 2163 email: secretary@meath.anglican.org

Cashel, Ferns and Ossory https://cashel.anglican.org

Bishop - A. M. Wilkinson, BA, MA, BTh, HDipEd [*Bishop's House, Troysgate, Kilkenny, R95 R2N1*] [Adrian Cashel Ferns and Ossory]

Deans - *Cashel*, J. G. Mulhall, DipSW, CQSW, BA; *Waterford*, B. J. Hayes; *Lismore*, P. R. Draper, BTh, MA; *Ossory (Kilkenny)*, S. A. Farrell, BA, MA, BTh, LLM; *Ferns*, P. G. Mooney, BD, ThM, DrTheol; *Leighlin*, T. W. Gordon, BEd, BTh, MA

Diocesan Secretary - E. Keyes, The Diocesan Office, The Palace Coach House, Church Lane, Kilkenny, R95 A032. Tel: 056 776 1910 email: office@cashel.anglican.org

Cork, Cloyne and Ross www.cork.anglican.org

Bishop - W. P. Colton, BCL, DipTh, MPhil, LLM, PhD [*St Nicholas House, 14 Cove Street, Cork, T12 RP40*] [Paul Cork]

Deans - *Cork*, N. K. Dunne, BA, BTh, MA, MPhil; *Cloyne*, S. D. Green, BA, HDipEd; *Ross*, C. P. Jeffers, BTh, MA

Diocesan and Glebes Secretary - W. G. Skuse, The Diocesan Office, St Nicholas House, 14 Cove Street, Cork, T12 RP40. Tel: 021 500 5080 email: secretary@corkchurchofireland.com and via website

Tuam, Limerick and Killaloe https://tlk.ie

Bishop - M. A. J. Burrows, BA, MA, MLitt, DipTh [*Kilbane House, Golf Links Road, Castletroy, Limerick*] [Michael Tuam, Limerick and Killaloe]

Deans - *Tuam* (*Vacant*) *Limerick*, N. J. W. Sloane, BA, MA, MPhil; *Killaloe* (*Vacant*)

Diocesan Administrator (*Tuam*) - H. Pope, 11 Ros Ard, Cappagh Road, Barna, Galway, H91 XW9A. Tel: 086 833 6666 email: secretary@tka.ie

Diocesan Secretary (*Limerick and Killaloe*) - L. Sharpe, Kellysgrove, Ballinasloe, Galway. Tel: 087 613 0063 email: diocesansecretary@limerick.anglican.org

The Churches of the Anglican Communion outside the British Isles

The Episcopal / Anglican Province of Alexandria

Archbishop of Alexandria and Bishop of Egypt - Samy Fawzy, Diocesan Office, PO Box 87, Zamalek Distribution 11211, Cairo, Egypt

The Anglican Church in Aotearoa, New Zealand and Polynesia

Primates and Archbishops - Don Tamihere, PO Box 568, Gisborne, 4040, New Zealand; Philip Richardson, PO Box 547, New Plymouth, 4621, New Zealand

The Anglican Church of Australia

Primate of Australia and Archbishop of Adelaide - Geoffrey Smith, 18 King William Road, North Adelaide, South Australia, 5006, Australia

Episcopal Church of Brazil (Igreja Episcopal Anglicana do Brasil)

Primate of Brazil and Bishop of Curitiba - Marinez Rosa Dos Santos Bassotto, Avenida Serzedelo Corrêa, 514 Batista Campos, Belem, PA, 66033-265, Brazil

The Anglican Church of Burundi

Archbishop of Burundi and Bishop of Makamba - Sixbert Macumi Nyaboho, BP 96, Makamba, Burundi

The Anglican Church of Canada

Primate of the Anglican Church of Canada - Linda Nicholls, 80 Hayden Street, Toronto, Ontario, M4Y 3G2, Canada

The Church of the Province of Central Africa

Archbishop of Central Africa and Bishop of Northern Zambia - Albert Chama, PO Box 22137, Kitwe, Zambia

The Anglican Church of the Central American Region (Iglesia Anglicana de la Region Central de America)

Primate of IARCA and Bishop of Panama - Juan David Alvarado Melgar, 7 Avenida Sur, 723 Col Flor Blanca, Apt Postal (01), San Salvador, 274, El Salvador

Iglesia Anglicana de Chile

Primate of the Anglican Church of Chile and Diocesan Bishop of Santiago - Hector Zavala, Casilla 50675, Correo Central, Santiago, Chile

The Anglican Church of the Province of Congo (Province de L'Eglise Anglicane du Congo)

Archbishop of the Congo and Bishop of Kindu - Titre Ande Georges, Avenue Penemisenga, No. 4, C/ Kasuku, Kindu Maniema, Rwanda

Hong Kong Sheng Kung Hui

Archbishop and Bishop of Western Kowloon - Andrew Chan, 11 Pak Po Street, Mongkok, Kowloon, Hong Kong, People's Republic of China

The Church of the Province of the Indian Ocean

Archbishop, Province of the Indian Ocean, and Bishop of the Seychelles - James Richard Wong Yin Song, Bishop's House, Bel Eau, Victoria, Mahé, Seychelles

The Nippon Sei Ko Kai (The Anglican Communion in Japan)

Primate of the NSKK and Bishop of Kyushu - Luke Kenichi Muto, 2-9-22 Kusagae, Chuo-ku, Fukuoka-shi, Fukuoka-ken, 810-0045, Japan

The Episcopal Church in Jerusalem and the Middle East

Primate of Jerusalem and the Middle East, Bishop in Cyprus and the Gulf - Michael Augustine Owen Lewis, Bishop's Office, PO Box 22075, CY 1517, Nicosia, Cyprus

The Anglican Church of Kenya

Primate and Archbishop of All Kenya - Jackson Ole Sapit, PO Box 40502, Nairobi, 100, Kenya

The Anglican Church of Korea

Primate of Korea and Bishop of Seoul - Peter Kyongho Lee, Bishop's Office, 16 Sejong-daero 19-gil, Jung-gu, Seoul, 100-120, Korea

The Anglican Church of Melanesia

Archbishop of the Anglican Church of Melanesia and Bishop of Central Melanesia - Leonard Dawea, Church of Melanesia, PO Box 19, Honiara, Solomon Islands

The Mexican Episcopal Church (La Iglesia Anglicana de Mexico)

Primate and Bishop of Cuernavaca - Enrique Treviño Cruz, Minerva #1, Fracc. Delicias, Cuernavaca, Morelos, 62330, Mexico

The Anglican Church of Mozambique and Angola (Igreja Anglicana de Mocambique e Angola)

Acting Presiding Bishop of Igreja Anglicana de Mocambique e Angola and Bishop of Lebombo - Carlos Simao Matsinhe, Caixa Postale 120, Maputo, Mozambique

The Church of the Province of Myanmar (Burma)

Archbishop of Myanmar and Bishop of Yangon - Stephen Than Myint Oo, No. 140 Pyidaungsu Yeiktha Street, PO Box 11191, Yangon, Myanmar

The Church of Nigeria (Anglican Communion)

Metropolitan and Primate of All Nigeria and Bishop of Abuja - Henry C. Ndukuba, St Matthias House, Plot 942 Gudu District, Abuja, Nigeria

The Anglican Church of Papua New Guinea

Bishop of Aipo and Acting Archbishop of Papua New Guinea - Nathan Ingen, PO Box 893, Mount Hagen, Western Highlands Province, Papua New Guinea

The Episcopal Church in the Philippines

Prime Bishop of the Philippines - Brent Alawas, Diocesan Office, Bontoc, Mt Province, 2616, Philippines

The Episcopal Church of Rwanda (L'Eglise Episcopal au Rwanda)

Archbishop of L'Eglise Episcopal au Rwanda and Bishop of Shyira - Laurent Mbanda, EER Shyira, PO Box 52, Ruhengeri, Rwanda

The Church of the Province of South East Asia

Archbishop of South East Asia and Bishop of Sabah - Melter Jiki Tais, PO Box 10811, 88809 Kota Kinabalu, Sabah, 88809 Malaysia

The Anglican Church of Southern Africa

Archbishop of Cape Town and Primate of Southern Africa - Thabo Makgoba, 20 Bishopscourt Drive, Bishopscourt, Claremont, Cape Town, Western Cape, 7708, South Africa

The Anglican Church of South America

Bishop of Northern Argentina and Primate of the Anglican Church of South America - Nicholas James Quested Drayson, Abraham Cornejo 120, 4400 Salta, Argentina

The Province of the Episcopal Church of Sudan

Archbishop of the Province of Sudan and Bishop of Khartoum - Ezekiel Kumir Kondo, PO Box 65, Omdurman, Sudan

The Province of the Episcopal Church of South Sudan

Archbishop and Primate of the Province of the Episcopal Church of South Sudan and Bishop of Juba - Justin Badi Arama, PO Box 110, Juba, South Sudan

The Anglican Church of Tanzania

Archbishop of Tanzania and Bishop of Tanga - Maimbo Mndolwa, PO Box 35, Korogwe, Tanga, Tanzania

The Church of the Province of Uganda

Archbishop of Uganda and Bishop of Mityana - Stephen Kaziimba, PO Box 102, Mityana, Uganda

The Episcopal Church in the United States of America

Presiding Bishop - Michael Curry, The Episcopal Church Center, 815 Second Avenue, New York, NY 10017, USA

The Church of the Province of West Africa

Primate of the CPWA and Bishop of Asante-Mampong - Cyril Kobina Ben-Smith, PO Box 220, Asante-Mampong, Ghana

The Church in the Province of the West Indies

Primate of the CPWI and Bishop of Jamaica and the Cayman Islands - Howard Gregory, Church House, 2 Caledonia Avenue, Cross Roads, Kingston 5, Jamaica

Attached to Canterbury:

The Anglican Church of Bermuda: Nicholas Dill

The Church of Ceylon: Keerthisiri Fernando

The Parish of the Falkland Islands: Jonathan Clark

The Lusitanian Church: José Jorge de Pina Cabral

The Reformed Episcopal Church of Spain: Carlos López-Lozano

Attached to the Episcopal Church in USA: Diocese of Taiwan, the Diocese of Puerto Rico and the Diocese of Venezuela

For details of the Anglican Consultative Council, which can provide further information from the Churches of the Anglican Communion outside the British Isles, please see below.

The Anglican Consultative Council

President – The Most Revd Justin P. Welby, Archbishop of Canterbury

Chair – The Most Revd Paul Kwong, Archbishop of Hong Kong Sheng Kung Hui and Bishop of Hong Kong Island

Vice-Chair – Canon Margaret Swinson

Secretary General – The Most Revd Dr Josiah Atkins Idowu-Fearon, the Anglican Consultative Council, the Anglican Communion Office, St Andrew's House, 16 Tavistock Crescent, London, W11 1AP. Tel: 020 7313 3903 email: secretary.general@aco.org

Anglican Centre in Rome – Director, The Most Revd Ian Ernest, Centro Anglicano, Palazzo Doria Pamphilj, Piazza del Collegio Romano 2, 00186 Rome, Italy email: administrator@anglicancentre.it

Churches with special relations to the Anglican Communion

The following Churches are in communion with all or some provinces of the Anglican Communion:

The Church of North India (United): Moderator – The Most Revd Bijay Nayak

The Church of Bangladesh: Moderator – The Most Revd Samuel Sunil Mankhin

The Church of Pakistan (United): Moderator – The Most Rt Revd Azad Marshall

The Church of South India (United): Moderator – The Most Revd Dharmaraj Rasalam

Mar Thoma Church (India): Metropolitan – The Most Revd Dr Theodosius Mar Thoma Metropolitan

Old Catholic Churches of The Union of Utrecht:

Netherlands: Archbishop of Utrecht – Bernd Wallet

Austria: Bishop – Heinz Lederleitner

Czech Republic: Bishop – Pavel B. Stránský

Germany: Bishop – Matthias Ring

Poland: Bishop – Wiktor Wysoczański

Switzerland: Bishop – Harald Rein

USA (Polish National Catholic Church): Prime Bishop – Anthony Mikovsky

Croatia: Bishop – Heinz Lederleitner

Philippine Independent Church: Supreme Bishop – Rhee M. Timbang

The Anglican Provinces in the British Isles and Ireland are in communication with some ***Lutheran Churches:***

Finland: Archbishop of Turku and Finland – Tapio Luoma

Iceland: Bishop – Agnes Sigurðardóttir

Norway: Presiding Bishop – Helga Haugland Byfuglien

Sweden: Archbishop of Uppsala – Antje Jackelén

Estonia: Archbishop - Urmas Viilma

Lithuania: Bishop - Mindaugas Sabutis

The World Council of Churches

General Secretary - The Revd Professor Jerry Pillay, PO Box 2100, CH-1211 Geneva 2, Switzerland.

Moderator of Central Committee - Dr Agnes Abuom

Ecumenical bodies

Churches Together in Britain and Ireland
https://ctbi.org.uk

Acting General Secretary - Dr Nicola Brady, Interchurch House, 35 Lower Marsh, London, SE1 7RL. Tel: 020 3794 2288 email: info@ctbi.org.uk

Churches Together in England
https://cte.org.uk

General Secretary - Bishop Mike Royal, 27 Tavistock Square, London, WC1H 9HH. Tel: 020 7529 8131 email: mike.royal@cte.org.uk

Action of Churches Together in Scotland (ACTS)
www.acts-scotland.org

General Secretary - The Revd Ian Boa (*Interim*), Jubilee House, Forthside Way, Stirling, FK8 1QZ.

CYTÛN: Churches Together in Wales
https://cytun.co.uk

Chief Executive - The Revd Aled Edwards, Room 3.3, Hastings House, Fitzalan Court, Cardiff, CF24 0BL. Tel: 07751 446071 email: aled@cytun.cymru

Irish Council of Churches
www.irishchurches.org

President - The Rt Revd Andrew Forster, Inter-Church Centre, 48 Elmwood Avenue, Belfast, BT9 6AZ. Tel: 028 9066 3145 email: info@irishchurches.org

The Church of England - central structures
www.churchofengland.org

The General Synod of the Church of England

Church House, Great Smith Street, London, SW1P 3AZ. Tel: 020 7898 1000 email: synod@churchofengland.org

Unless otherwise indicated, all addresses in this section are as above. Email addresses generally follow the pattern christianname.surname@churchofengland.org

Secretary General - William Nye, Tel: 020 7898 1361

Principal commissions

The Clergy Discipline Commission

Secretary Conor Gannon

The Crown Nominations Commission

Secretary Canon Caroline Boddington

The Dioceses Commission

Secretary Jenny Axtell

The Faith and Order Commission

Secretary Canon Jeremy Worthen

The Fees Advisory Commission

Secretary Suzanne Esson

The Legal Advisory Commission

Secretary The Revd Alexander McGregor

The Legal Aid Commission

Secretary Stephen York

The Liturgical Commission

Secretary Sue Moore

The Archbishops' Council

(and Central Board of Finance of the Church of England)
Church House, Great Smith Street, London, SW1P 3AZ
Tel: 020 7898 1000

Unless otherwise indicated, all addresses in this section are as above. Email addresses generally follow the pattern christianname.surname@churchofengland.org

Secretary General – William Nye, Tel: 020 7898 1360

The Appointments Committee of the Church of England

Secretary Stephen Knott, Tel: 020 7898 1363

Cathedral and Church Buildings Division

Director Becky Clark

The Church Buildings Council

Chair Jennifer Page, Tel: 020 7898 1000

Central Secretariat

Clerk to the Synod and Director of Central Secretariat for the Archbishops' Council

Simon Gallagher, Tel: 020 7898 1000

The Council for Christian Unity

Secretary for Ecumenical Relations and Theology

The Revd Prebendary Dr Isabelle Hamley, Tel: 020 7898 1228

Head of Research and Statistics

Dr Ken Eames

Communications Office

Director of Communications

Mark Arena, Tel: 020 7898 1000

Church House Publishing

Publishing Manager

Dr Thomas Allain Chapman, Tel: 01603 785 925

Education Office

Chief Education Officer

The Revd Nigel Genders, Tel: 020 7898 1000

Evangelism and Discipleship

Director Dave Male

Finance Division

Finance Committee

Secretary David White, Tel: 020 7898 1000

Audit and Risk Committee

Secretary Stephanie Harrison, Tel: 020 7898 1000

Human Resources Department

Director Christine Hewitt-Dyer, Tel: 020 7989 1000

The Legal Office

Head of the Legal Office, Chief Legal Adviser to the Archbishops' Council and the General Synod and Official Solicitor to the Church Commissioners

The Revd Alexander McGregor, Tel: 020 7898 1722

Ministry Division

Director of Ministry

The Rt Revd Chris Goldsmith, Tel: 020 7898 1000

The Central Readers' Council

Secretary Andrew Walker, Tel: 020 7898 1417

Mission and Public Affairs Division

Director The Revd Canon Dr Malcolm Brown, Tel: 020 7898 1468

Hospital Chaplaincies Administrator Mary Ingledew, Tel: 020 7898 1000

Committee for Minority Ethnic Anglican Concerns

Chair The Very Revd Rogers Govender MBE

Racial Justice Unit

Director The Revd Guy Hewitt, Tel: 020 7898 1000

Renewal and Reform

Director Debbie Clinton

Setting God's People Free

Programme Director Dr Nick Shepherd

Tel: 020 7898 1000

The Church Commissioners for England

Church House, Great Smith Street,
London, SW1P 3AZ
Tel: 020 7898 1000

Secretary and Chief Executive Gareth Mostyn, Tel: 020 7898 1000

The Three Church Estates Commissioners – Alan Smith, Andrew Selous, MP, Canon Flora Winfield

The Church of England Pensions Board

29 Great Smith Street, London, SW1P 3PS
Tel: 020 7898 1000
Chief Executive Clive Mather, Tel: 020 7898 1000

Other boards, councils, commissions, etc., of the Church of England

The Churches Conservation Trust

Chief Executive Greg Pickup, Unit G41 c/o Vulcan Works, 34–38 Guildhall Road, Northampton, NN1 1EW. Tel: 0845 303 2760

The Corporation of the Church House

Secretary Stephanie Maurel, Church House, 27 Great Smith Street, London, SW1P 3AZ. Tel: 020 7898 1311

Theological colleges of the Church of England

College of the Resurrection, Stocks Bank Road, Mirfield, WF14 0BW.
https://college.mirfield.org.uk Tel: 01924 490441
email: alewis@mirfield.org.uk
Principal, The Rt Revd M. C. R. Sowerby, BD, MA, AKC

Cranmer Hall (St John's College), 3 South Bailey, Durham, DH1 3RJ.
https://cranmerhall.com Tel: 0191 334 3894
email: cranmer.admissions@durham.ac.uk
Warden, The Revd Dr P. J. J. Plyming, BA, PhD

Emmanuel Theological College, 7 Abbey Square, Chester, CH1 2HU. https://emmanueltheologicalcollege.org.uk
email: info@emmanueltheologicalcollege.org.uk
Dean, The Revd Dr M. Leyden

Oak Hill College, Chase Side, Southgate, London, N14 4PS.
www.oakhill.ac.uk Tel: 020 8449 0467 email: via website
President, The Revd J. S. Juckes, BA, MA

The Queen's Foundation for Ecumenical Theological Education, Somerset Road, Edgbaston, Birmingham, B15 2QH.
www.queens.ac.uk Tel: 0121 454 1527 email: enquire@queens.ac.uk
Principal, Professor C. Marsh, BA, DPhil, MEd

Ridley Hall, Ridley Hall Road, Cambridge, CB3 9HG.
www.ridley.cam.ac.uk Tel: 01223 746580
email: info@ridley.cam.ac.uk
Principal, The Revd Dr M. J. Volland, BA, MA, DThM

Ripon College Cuddesdon, Cuddesdon, Oxford, OX44 9EX.
www.rcc.ac.uk Tel: 01865 877404 email: enquiries@rcc.ac.uk
Principal, The Rt Revd H. I. J. Southern, BA, MA

St Mellitus College, London, 24 Collingham Road, London, SW5 0LX.
https://stmellitus.ac.uk Tel: 020 7052 0573
email: info@stmellitus.ac.uk
Dean, The Revd R. J. Winfield, BA, BTh, MA

St Stephen's House, 16 Marston Street, Oxford, OX4 1JX.
www.ssho.ox.ac.uk Tel: 01865 613500
email: enquiries@ssho.ox.ac.uk
Principal, The Revd Canon Dr R. Ward, BA, MA, PhD

The Sarum Centre for Formation in Ministry and Training, Sarum College, 19 The Close, Salisbury, SP1 2EE. www.sarum.ac.uk/ministry/ Tel: 01722 424800 email: info@sarum.ac.uk *Principal*, The Revd Canon Professor J. W. Woodward, BD, AKC, STh, MPhil, PhD, FRSA

Trinity College, Stoke Hill, Stoke Bishop, Bristol, BS9 1JP. www.trinitycollegebristol.ac.uk Tel: 0117 968 2803 email: reception@trinitycollegebristol.ac.uk *Principal*, The Revd Dr S. Doherty, BA, MPhil, DPhil

Westcott House, Jesus Lane, Cambridge, CB5 8BP. www.westcott.cam.ac.uk Tel: 01223 741000 email: info@westcott.cam.ac.uk *Principal,* The Revd Dr H. E. Dawes, BA, MA

Wycliffe Hall, 54 Banbury Road, Oxford, OX2 6PW. www.wycliffehall.ox.ac.uk Tel: 01865 274200 email: via website *Principal,* The Revd Dr M. F. Lloyd, BA, MA, DPhil

Theological training: part-time courses

Cuddesdon Gloucester and Hereford, 12 College Green, Gloucester, GL1 2LX. www.rcc.ac.uk/ordination-training/part-time-pathways/cuddesdon-gloucester-hereford-cgh Tel: 01452 874969 email: GloucesterHereford@rcc.ac.uk *Director*, The Revd Dr R. A. Latham

Eastern Region Ministry Course, ERMC, 1a The Bounds, Westminster College, Lady Margaret Road, Cambridge, CB3 0BJ. www.ermc.cam.ac.uk Tel: 01223 760 444 email: admin@ermc.cam.ac.uk *Principal,* The Revd Dr A. Jensen

Emmanuel Theological College, 7 Abbey Square, Chester, CH1 2HU. https://emmanueltheologicalcollege.org.uk email: info@emmanueltheologicalcollege.org.uk *Dean*, The Revd Dr M. Leyden

Midlands Ministry Training Course, Midlands Gospel Partnership, c/o Stapleford Baptist, Albert Street, Stapleford, Nottingham, NG9 8DB. https://midlandsgospel.org.uk Tel: 0121 454 9444 email: admin@midlandsgospel.org.uk *Director of Training,* P. Hancock

Oak Hill College, Chase Side, Southgate, London, N14 4PS. https://oakhill.ac.uk Tel: 020 8449 0467 email: via website *President*, The Revd J. S. Juckes

Ripon College Cuddeson Part-Time Pathway, Ripon College Cuddesdon, Cuddesdon, Oxford, OX44 9EX. www.rcc.ac.uk/ordination-training/part-time-pathways/ripon-college-cuddesdon-part-time-pathway-ptp Tel: 01865 877404 email: admissions@rcc.ac.uk *Director*, Revd Dr S. Snyder

St Augustine's College of Theology, 52 Swan Street, West Malling, Kent, ME19 6JX. https://staugustinescollege.ac.uk Tel: 01732 252656 email: via website or admissions@staugustinescollege.ac.uk *Principal,* The Revd Dr A. Gregory

St Hild College, Stocks Bank Road, Mirfield WF14 0BW. https://sthild.org Tel: 01924 481925 email: enquiries@sthild.org and via website *Principal*, The Revd Canon Dr M. Powley

The Sarum Centre for Formation in Ministry, Sarum College, 19 The Close, Salisbury, SP1 2EE. www.sarum.ac.uk/ministry/ Tel: 01722 424820 email: info@sarum.ac.uk *Principal*, The Revd Canon Professor J. Woodward

South West Ministry Training Course, SWMTC, Riverside Church and Conference Centre, 13–14 Okehampton Street, St Thomas, Exeter, EX4 1DU. https://swmtc.org.uk Tel: 01392 272544 email: admin@swmtc.org.uk *Principal*, The Revd Dr M. A. Butchers

Religious societies, institutions and publications

Further information on mission agencies may be obtained from Partnership for World Mission
(see address on page 301)

Additional Curates Society https://additionalcurates.co.uk
General Secretary, Fr D. Smith, Additional Curates Society, 16 Commercial Street, Birmingham, B1 1RS. Tel: 0121 382 5533 email: info@additionalcurates.co.uk

Alcuin Club https://alcuinclub.org.uk *Chairman,* The Revd Canon C. Irvine, 5 Saffron Street, Royston, SG8 9TR. Tel: 01763 248676 email: alcuinclub@gmail.com

Anglican and Eastern Churches Association https://aeca.org.uk
Chairman, The Revd Canon Dr W. Taylor, St John's Vicarage, 25 Ladbroke Road, London, W11 3PD. Tel: 020 7727 4262 email: chairman@aeca.org.uk

Anglican Centre in Rome, The www.anglicancentreinrome.org
Development Officer UK, C. Pepinster, c/o The Anglican Communion Office, St Andrew's House, 16 Tavistock Crescent, London, W11 1AP. Tel: 07719 534084 email: development@anglicancentre.it

Anglican Pacifist Fellowship www.anglicanpeacemaker.org.uk
APF Coordinator, T. Martin, Peace House, 19 Paradise Street, Oxford, OX1 1LD. email: tilly@anglicanpeacemaker.org.uk

Anglican Society for the Welfare of Animals, The www.aswa.org.uk
Chair, The Revd Dr H. Hall, PO Box 7193, Hook, Hampshire, RG27 8GT. Tel: 01252 843093 email: angsocwelanimals@aol.com

Association of Interchurch Families www.interchurchfamilies.org.uk
Executive Development Officer, D. Hayes, 3rd Floor, 20 King Street, London, EC2V 8EG. Tel: 020 3384 2947 email: info@interchurchfamilies.org.uk

Baptists Together www.baptist.org.uk
General Secretary, L. Green, Baptist House, PO Box 44, 129 Broadway, Didcot, OX11 8RT. Tel: 01235 517700 email: via website

Bible Reading Fellowship www.brf.org.uk
Chief Executive, R. Fisher, 15 The Chambers, Vineyard, Abingdon, OX14 3FE. Tel: 01865 319700 email: enquiries@brf.org.uk and via website

Bible Society www.biblesociety.org.uk *Chief Executive,* P. Williams, Stonehill Green, Westlea, Swindon, SN5 7DG. Tel: 01793 418222 email: via website

Boys' Brigade, The https://boys-brigade.org.uk *Chief Executive,* J. Eales, Felden Lodge, Hemel Hempstead, HP3 0BL. Tel: 0300 303 4454 email: support@boys-brigade.org.uk

Catholic Church in England and Wales, The www.cbcew.org.uk
General Secretary, The Revd Canon C. Thomas, Catholic Bishops' Conference of England and Wales, 39 Eccleston Square, London, SW1V 1BX. email: via website

CHRISM: CHRistians in Secular Ministry https://chrism.org.uk
Secretary, M. Trivasse. Tel: 07796 366220 email: margtriv@yahoo.co.uk

Children's Society, The www.childrenssociety.org.uk
Chief Executive, M. Russell, Whitecross Studios, 50 Banner Street, London, EC1Y 8ST. Tel: 0300 303 7000 email: supportercare@childrenssociety.org.uk

Christian Aid www.christianaid.org.uk *Chief Executive,* P. Watt, 35–41 Lower Marsh, Waterloo, London, SE1 7RL. Tel: 020 7620 4444 email: via website

Christian Evidence Society https://christianevidencesociety.org.uk *Chair*, E. Carter. email: via website

Christians Abroad www.cabroad.org.uk *Chair*, A. Wileman, 399 Ringwood Road, Ferndown, Dorset, BH22 9AF. Tel: 0300 012 1201 email: support@cabroad.org.uk

Church Army https://churcharmy.org *Chief Executive Officer,* P. Rouch, Church Army, Wilson Carlile Centre, 50 Cavendish Street, Sheffield, S3 7RZ. Tel: 0300 123 2113 email: via website

Churches Conservation Trust, The www.visitchurches.org.uk *Chief Executive,* G. Pickup, Unit G41 c/o Vulcan Works, 34–38 Guildhall Road, Northampton, NN1 1EW. Tel: 0845 303 2760 email: via website

Church Lads' and Church Girls' Brigade www.clcgb.org.uk *Governor,* A. Hayday, St Martin's House, 2 Barnsley Road, Wath-upon-Dearne, Rotherham, S63 6PY. Tel: 01709 876535 email: contactus@clcgb.org.uk

Church Mission Society https://churchmissionsociety.org *CEO*, A. Bateman, Watlington Road, Oxford, OX4 6BZ. Tel: 01865 787400 email: via website

Church Music Society https://church-music.org.uk *Honorary Secretary,* Dr S. Lindley email: webenquiries@church-music.org.uk

Church of England Communications Office www.churchofengland.org/media-and-news/media-centre/communications-team *Director of Communications*, M. Arena, Church House, Great Smith Street, London, SW1P 3AZ. Tel: 020 7898 1326 email: via website

Church of England Education Office See *National Society for Promoting Religious Education*

Church of England Evangelical Council https://ceec.info *Co-chairs,* The Revd L. Goddard and E. Shaw email: via website

Church of England Newspaper, The www.churchnewspaper.com *Editor,* A. Carey, Political and Religious Intelligence Ltd, 14 Great College Street, Westminster, London, SW1P 3RX. Tel: 020 7222 2018 email: andrew.carey@churchnewspaper.com

Church of Scotland https://churchofscotland.org.uk *Moderator*, I. Greenshields 121 George Street, Edinburgh, EH2 4YN. Tel: 0131 225 5722 email: via website

Church Pastoral Aid Society (CPAS) www.cpas.org.uk *Chief Executive Officer*, The Revd J. L. Scamman, Sovereign Court One (Unit 3), Sir William Lyons Road, University of Warwick Science Park, Coventry, CV4 7EZ. Tel: 0300 123 0780 email: info@cpas.org.uk and via website

Church Society www.churchsociety.org *Director,* The Revd Dr L. Gatiss, Ground Floor, Centre Block, Hille Business Estate, 132 St Albans Road, Watford, WD24 4AE. Tel: 01923 255410 email: via website

Church Times www.churchtimes.co.uk *Managing Editor*, P. Handley, 3rd Floor, Invicta House, 108–114 Golden Lane, London, EC1Y 0TG. Tel: 020 7776 1060 email: editor@churchtimes.co.uk

Church Urban Fund https://cuf.org.uk *Executive Director*, R. Whittington, The Foundry, 17 Oval Way, London, SE11 5RR. Tel: 0203 752 5655 email: hello@cuf.org.uk

Church's Ministry among Jewish People, The (CMJ UK) www.cmj.org.uk *Chief Executive Officer,* The Revd A. Jacob, Eagle Lodge, Hexgreave Hall Business Park, Farnsfield, Nottinghamshire, NG22 8LS. Tel: 01623 883960 email: office@cmj.org.uk and via website

Clergy Support Trust www.clergysupport.org.uk *Chief Executive Officer*, The Revd B. Cahill-Nicholls, 1 Dean Trench Street, Westminster, London, SWIP 3HB. Tel: 0800 389 5192 email: via website

College of Health Care Chaplains www.healthcarechaplains.org *Registrar*, A. Dean, CHCC/Unite,128 Theobald's Road, London, WC1X 8TN. Tel: 01792 703301 email: Allison.Dean@unitetheunion.org

Confraternity of The Blessed Sacrament https://confraternity.org.uk *Secretary General*, The Revd E. Martin, c/o The ACS, 16 Commercial Street, Birmingham, B1 1RS. email: admin@confraternity.org.uk

Congregational Federation www.congregational.org.uk *General Secretary*, Y. Campbell, 8 Castle Gate, Nottingham, NG1 7AS. Tel: 0115 911 1460 email: via website

Council of Christians and Jews, The https://ccj.org.uk *Co-Director,* The Revd Dr N. Eddy and Georgina Bye, Faith House, 7 Tufton Street, London, SW1P 3QB. Tel: 020 3515 3003 email: via website

Crosslinks www.crosslinks.org *Mission Director,* J. McLernon, 251 Lewisham Way, London, SE4 1XF. Tel: 020 8691 6111 email: info@crosslinks.org

Ecclesiastical Insurance Group www.ecclesiastical.com *Managing Director UK*, Richard Coleman, Benefact House, 2000 Pioneer Avenue, Gloucester Business Park, Brockworth, Gloucester, GL3 4AW. Tel: 0345 777 3322 email: information@ecclesiastical.com

Ecclesiastical Law Society https://ecclawsoc.org.uk *Executive Secretary,* The Rt Revd J. F. Ford, 1 The Sanctuary, London, SW1P 3JT. email: admin@ecclawsoc.org.uk and via website

English Clergy Association, The www.clergyassoc.co.uk *Chairman*, Dr P. M. Smith, 36 High Street, Silverton, Exeter, EX5 4JD. Tel: 01392 860284 email: p.m.smith@exeter.ac.uk

Feed the Minds www.feedtheminds.org *CEO,* S. Golding, The Foundry, 17 Oval Way, London, SE11 5RR. Tel: 020 3752 5800 email: info@feedtheminds.org

Fellowship of Contemplative Prayer, The www.contemplative-prayer.org.uk *Chair*, The Revd J. C. Hill email: admin@contemplative-prayer.org.uk

Fellowship of St Alban and St Sergius https://fsass.org *General Secretary,* Fr S. Platt, 1 Canterbury Road, Oxford, OX2 6LU. Tel: 01865 552 991 email: gensec@sobornost.org

Forward in Faith https://forwardinfaith.com *Director,* T. Middleton, St Andrew Holborn, 5 St Andrew Street, London, EC4A 3AF. Tel: 07368 124811 email: director@forwardinfaith.com

Girls Friendly Society https://girlsfriendlysociety.org.uk *Chief Executive Officer*, L. Sercombe, Unit 12 Angel Gate, London, EC1V 2PT. Tel: 020 7837 9669 email: info@girlsfriendlysociety.org.uk

Girlguiding www.girlguiding.org.uk *Chief Executive*, A. Salt, 17–19 Buckingham Palace Road, London, SW1W 0PT. Tel: 0800 999 2016 email: via website

Girls' Brigade England & Wales, The www.girlsb.org.uk *Director*, J. Murdy, Cliff College, Calver, Hope Valley, Derbyshire, S32 3XG. Tel: 01246 582322 email: gbco@gb-ministries.org

Guild of All Souls, The www.guildofallsouls.org.uk *General Secretary*, C. Sherwood, Dalton House, 60 Windsor Avenue, London, SW19 2RR. Tel: 07498 778691 email: guildofallsouls@outlook.com and via website

Guild of Church Musicians, The www.churchmusicians.org *President*, Dame M. Archer, 3 Sewards End, Wickford, Essex, SS12 9PB. email: via website

Guild of Health and St Raphael, The https://gohealth.org.uk *Director*, The Revd Dr G. Straine, 23 The Close, Lichfield, WS13 7LD. email: via website

Guild of Servants of the Sanctuary https://guildofservantsofthesanctuary.co.uk *Secretary General*, M. Andrew, c/o ACS, 16 Commercial Street, Birmingham, B1 1RS. email: gss.secretarygeneral@gmail.com and via website

Guild of Vergers, The Church of England https://cofegv.org.uk *General Secretary*, S. Stokes, 124 City Road, London, EC1V 2NX. email: CEGVGenSec@gmail.com

Hymn Society of Great Britain and Ireland, The https://hymnsocietygbi.org.uk *Honorary Secretary*, The Revd R. A. Canham, Windrush, Braithwaite, Keswick, CA12 5SZ. Tel: 0176 877 8054 email: via website

ICF (Industrial Christian Fellowship) www.icf-online.org *Secretary*, A. Wright, The Resource Centre, Fleet Street, Wigan, WN5 0DS. email: admin@icf-online.org

Intercontinental Church Society www.ics-uk.org *Mission Director*, R. Bromley, Unit 11, Ensign Business Centre, Westwood Way, Westwood Business Park, Coventry, CV4 8JA. email: via website

Jerusalem and Middle East Church Association www.jmeca.org.uk *Secretary*, S. Eason, 1 Hart House, The Hart, Farnham, Surrey, GU9 7HJ. Tel: 01252 726994 email: information@jmeca.org.uk

Keston Institute www.keston.org.uk *Chair*, X. Dennen, 47 South Street, Durham, DH1 4QP. email: administrator@keston.org.uk and via website

Leprosy Mission, The www.leprosymission.org.uk *National Director*, P. Waddup, Goldhay Way, Orton Goldhay, Peterborough, PE2 5GZ. Tel: 01733 370505 email: via website

Lesbian and Gay Christian Movement www.onebodyonefaith.org.uk *Executive Director*, L. Dowding. Tel: 01636 673072 email: via website

Methodist Church, The www.methodist.org.uk *Secretary of the Conference*, The Revd Dr J. Hustler, Methodist Church House, 25 Marylebone Road, London, NW1 5JR. Tel: 020 7467 5157 email: soc@methodistchurch.org.uk

Mission to Seafarers, The www.missiontoseafarers.org *Secretary General*, A. Wright, 1st floor, 6 Bath Place, Rivington Street, London, EC2A 3JE. Tel: 020 7248 5202 email: via website

Modern Church www.modernchurch.org.uk *General Secretary*, A. Webster, Modern Church, 22 The Kiln, Burgess Hill, West Sussex, RH15 0LU. Tel: 0845 345 1909 email: via website

Moravian Church British Province, The www.moravian.org.uk *Administrator*, L. Newens, Moravian Church House, 5 Muswell Hill, London, N10 3TJ. Tel: 020 8883 3409 email: office@moravian.org.uk and via website

Mothers' Union www.mothersunion.org *Chief Executive*, B. Jullien, Mary Sumner House, 24 Tufton Street, London, SW1P 3RB. Tel: 020 7222 5533 email: via website

National Churches Trust www.nationalchurchestrust.org *Chief Executive*, C. Walker, 7 Tufton Street, London, SW1P 3QB. Tel: 020 7222 0605 email: info@nationalchurchestrust.org and via website

National Society for Promoting Religious Education, The www.churchofengland.org/about/education-and-schools/education-contacts *Chief Education Officer,* N. Genders, Church House, Great Smith Street, London, SW1P 3AZ. Tel: 020 7898 1219 email: gaylene.smith@churchofengland.org or via website

Open Synod Group www.opensynodgroup.org.uk *Chair*, P. Allen. email: mrspennyallen@yahoo.co.uk

Orthodox Church http://sgois.co.uk St George Orthodox Information Service, The White House, Mettingham, NR35 1TP. Tel: 01986 895176 email: stgeorgeois@aol.com and via website

Partnership for World Mission www.churchofengland.org/resources/world-mission Church House, Great Smith Street, London, SW1P 3AZ. Tel: 020 7898 1000 email: via website

Prayer Book Society, The www.pbs.org.uk *Company Secretary*, F. Rosen, The Studio, Copyhold Farm, Lady Grove, Goring Heath, Reading, RG8 7RT. Tel: 0118 984 2582 email: pbs.admin@pbs.org.uk

Prison Fellowship https://prisonfellowship.org.uk *Chief Executive Officer*, P. Holloway, PO Box 68226, London, SW1P 9WR. Tel: 020 7799 2500 email: info@prisonfellowship.org.uk and via website

Quakers in Britain www.quaker.org.uk Friends House, 173 Euston Road, London, NW1 2BJ. Tel: 020 7663 1000 email: enquiries@quaker.org.uk

Radius (The Religious Drama Society of Great Britain) 4 Carpenter Avenue, Llandudno, LL30 1YW. www.radiusdrama.org.uk email: info@radius.org.uk and via website

Retreat Association, The www.retreats.org.uk *Director*, A. MacTier, PO Box 1130, Princes Risborough, Buckinghamshire, HP22 9RP. Tel: 01494 569 056 email: info@retreats.org.uk and via website

Royal School of Church Music, The www.rscm.org.uk *Director*, H. Morris, 19 The Close, Salisbury, Wiltshire, SP1 2EB. Tel: 01722 424848 email: enquiries@rscm.com and via website

Rural Theology Association, The https://ruraltheologyassociation.com *Secretary*, The Revd A. Stevenson email: via website

St Luke's for Clergy Wellbeing www.stlukesforclergy.org.uk *Chief Executive*, Dr C. Walker, Room 201, Church House, Great Smith Street, London, SW1P 3AZ. Tel: 020 4546 7000 email: enquiries@stlukesforclergy.org.uk and via website

St Marylebone Healing and Counselling Centre https://marylebone-hcc.org.uk *Director of Clinical Services*, S. Hyde, 17 Marylebone Road, London, NW1 5LT. Tel: 020 7935 5066 email: healing@stmarylebone.org

Salvation Army, The www.salvationarmy.org.uk *Commissioners*, A. and G. Cotterill, Territorial Headquarters, 101 Newington Causeway, London, SE1 6BN. Tel: 020 7367 4500 email: info@salvationarmy.org.uk

Scout Association, The www.scouts.org.uk *Chief Executive*, M.Hyde, Gilwell Park, Chingford, London, E4 7QW. Information Centre: 0345 300 1818 email: info.centre@scouts.org.uk

Scripture Union www.scriptureunion.org.uk *National Director,* M. MacBean, Trinity House, Opal Court, Opal Drive, Fox Milne, Milton Keynes, MK15 0DF. Tel: 01908 856000 email: hello@scriptureunion.org.uk and via website

Servants of Christ the King www.sck.org.uk *Church Administrator*, S. Bennett, Christ the Servant King Church, Sycamore Road, High Wycombe, Bucks, HP12 4TJ. Tel: 01494 459070 email: office@sck.org.uk and via website

Society for Promoting Christian Knowledge, The *See page 302.*

Student Christian Movement www.movement.org.uk *Chief Executive Officer*, The Revd N. Nixon, Grays Court, 3 Nursery Road, Edgbaston, Birmingham, B15 3JX. Tel: 0121 426 4918 email: scm@movement.org.uk

Theatre Chaplaincy UK https://theatrechaplaincyuk.com *Senior Chaplain,* The Revd L. Meader, St Paul's Church, Bedford Street, London, WC2E 9ED. Tel: 07501 829491 email: info@theatrechaplaincyuk.com

Theology (the journal) https://journals.sagepub.com/home/TJX *Editor*, R. Gill, Sage Publications Ltd, 1 Oliver's Yard, 55 City Road, London, EC1Y 1SP. Tel: 020 7324 8500 email: theology@spck.org.uk

Toc H www.toch-uk.org.uk *Chief Executive Officer*, P. Hackwood, 483 Green Lanes, London, N13 4BS. Tel: 0121 443 3552 email: info@toch.org.uk

UCCF: The Christian Unions www.uccf.org.uk *Director,* R. Cunningham, Blue Boar House, 5 Blue Boar Street, Oxford, OX1 4EE. Tel: 01865 253678 email: info@uccf.org.uk

United Reformed Church, The https://urc.org.uk *General Secretary,* The Revd Dr J. Bradbury, United Reformed Church House, 86 Tavistock Place, London, WC1H 9RT. Tel: 020 7916 2020 email: urc@urc.org.uk and via website

USPG https://uspg.org.uk *General Secretary,* Revd Dr D. Dormor, 5 Trinity Street, London, SE1 1DB. Tel: 020 7921 2200 email: info@uspg.org.uk

WATCH (Women and the Church) https://womenandthechurch.org *Chair,* Revd M. Oborne, PO Box 75, Upper Rissington, Cheltenham, GL54 2XR. email: admin@womenandthechurch.org

Week of Prayer for World Peace https://weekofprayerforworldpeace.co.uk 112 Whittlesey Road, March, PE15 0AH. Tel: 07964 216480 email: wpwp2021@yahoo.com

Women's World Day of Prayer www.wwdp.org.uk *Administrator,* V. Daniell, Commercial Road, Tunbridge Wells, Kent, TN1 2RR. Tel: 01892 541411 email: via website

YMCA www.ymca.org.uk *Chief Executive Officer and National Secretary*, D. Hatton, YMCA England and Wales, 10–11 Charterhouse Square, London, EC1M 6EH. Tel: 020 7186 9500 email: enquiries@ymca.org.uk

Young Women's Trust www.youngwomenstrust.org *Chief Executive*, C. Reindorp, Unit D, 15–18 White Lion Street, London, N1 9PD. Tel: 020 7837 2019 email: contact@youngwomenstrust.org and via website

The Society for Promoting Christian Knowledge

Founded in 1698.

36 Causton Street, London, SW1P 4ST

Telephone: 020 7592 3900 email: spck@spck.org.uk and via website

website: www.spck.org.uk

SPCK is the Anglican mission agency working through publishing. Our vision is creating conversations between Christianity and culture. Our mission is publishing great Christian books around the world. We are committed to sharing innovative Christian thinking to enable people of all backgrounds to increase their understanding of the Christian faith. SPCK publishes under a range of imprints, including SPCK, Marylebone House, Inter-Varsity Press, Apollos, Monarch, Lion, Candle and York Courses. Each year, we sell half a million books and apps; our books have been translated into 88 languages; we have 50,000 web visitors every month. Profits from sales of these books are used to support our programmes, such as the free Assemblies website (www.Assemblies.org.uk), the free Home Groups website (www.HomeGroups.org.uk), the African Theological Network Press and Diffusion Prison Fiction. We also work with Clergy Support Trust to make available the Clergy Support Trust library, containing more than a thousand e-books and free to all ordinands and curates.

Memoranda

Memoranda

Addresses

Name

Address

Telephone

Mobile

Email

Name

Address

Telephone

Mobile

Email

Name

Address

Telephone

Mobile

Email

Addresses

Name

Address

Telephone

Mobile

Email

Name

Address

Telephone

Mobile

Email

Name

Address

Telephone

Mobile

Email

Addresses

Name

Address

Telephone

Mobile

Email

Name

Address

Telephone

Mobile

Email

Name

Address

Telephone

Mobile

Email

Addresses

Name

Address

Telephone

Mobile

Email

Name

Address

Telephone

Mobile

Email

Name

Address

Telephone

Mobile

Email

Addresses

Name

Address

Telephone

Mobile

Email

Name

Address

Telephone

Mobile

Email

Name

Address

Telephone

Mobile

Email